Without Saints

Without Saints

Essays

Christopher Locke

www.blacklawrence.com

Executive Editor: Diane Goettel
Cover Design: Zoe Norvell
Cover Art: "Fear of Flying" by Amelia Bernays Pitti
Book Design: Amy Freels

Published 2022 by Black Lawrence Press.

Excerpts from the following poems are used by permission of the authors and/or publishers:
"Wheels" by Jim Daniels
"To Myself" by Franz Wright
"Rain" (poem) from *The Far Mosque* by Kazim Ali, Alice James Books, 2005.
Tony Hoagland, excerpt from "I Have Good News" from *Priest Turned Therapist Treats Fear of God*. Copyright © 2018 by Tony Hoagland. Reprinted with the permission of The Permissions Company, LLC on behalf of Graywolf Press, Minneapolis, Minnesota, www.graywolfpress.org.

Acknowledgments

I am grateful to the editors of the following magazines where some of these essays first appeared, often in different forms:
Atticus Review: "Call My Name"; *Barnstorm*: "Unforgivable"; *Book of Matches*: "The Weight of Fire"; *EX/POST*: "Voice"; *Jet Fuel Review*: "Corrections"; *JMWW*: "Friction"; *Love in the Time of Covid* (New Zealand): "Beacon"; *(mac)ro(mic)*: "Pieces"; *MoonPark Review*: "With You"; *Poets & Writers*: "Fleeting"; *The Rumpus*: "The Night Faerie"; *The Rush*: "Another Life"; *The Sun*: "Possessed"

Contents

For my family: blood and otherwise

"We are made to persist. That's how we find out who we are."

—Tobias Wolff

Pieces

When my mother was eight years old, she climbed to the top of her neighbor's greenhouse and leapt, convinced she would fly. Her body crashed through the glass and she landed on top of a table filled with bright yellow daffodils.

Her right calf was badly cut, and after her neighbors rushed out to help her off the crumpled flowers and pick the glass out of her hair, they wrapped her leg, called her mom, and sent her home.

My mom limped across the street and bled up the stairs of her house in Hull, Massachusetts. Her mom attended to her wound and when her father returned from work, he pointed out all the blood still on the porch and said do you know how this makes us look?

*   *   *

At night, my mother lay motionless in her bed and listened very carefully. Sometimes she was alone. Sometimes one or all of her sisters were with her. They waited to hear the stairs. They waited to see who their father would choose.

*   *   *

When my mom was sixteen, she sat in the back of her parents' Oldsmobile as her mother drove. They were going to the pharmacy to buy pantyhose. About halfway there, her mom pulled over on the side of the road, blinker ticking. She turned around and faced my mother.

"You're a little whore," she said, and slapped my mother across the face.

She then turned back around, checked her mirrors, and continued to the pharmacy where they were having a sale on Hanes, the leading brand of pantyhose in 1964.

*   *   *

My mother met my father in Boston when she was seventeen. They were both attending a small communications school. My father had just returned from Korea after two years in the Army. He had been a journalist with *Stars and Stripes* and once blundered into the DMZ, almost causing an international incident. He now wanted to be a disc jockey. My mother dreamt of becoming an actress. My mom, who still lived at home, was soon pregnant. When my father asked if they should get married, move up to New Hampshire to be closer to his family, my mother smiled.

*   *   *

After my brother was born, my mother went to see the doctor for her first postpartum checkup. The doctor said she seemed healthy, asked how the baby was. My mother said he was good. "Great," he said. "Because you're pregnant again." And I was born the following October.

*   *   *

When I was eighteen, my mother remarried. That Thanksgiving, she invited her father over. She also invited her sisters. They were all waiting for him. We had a kind of dinner. Afterward, I snuck beers and drank them in my bedroom with my brother, who was on leave from the Marines. We listened very carefully. We heard many voices rise into a single knot in the dining room. As I looked out my bedroom window and watched my grandfather drive away, I understood I would never see him again.

Weeks later, setting up the Christmas tree, my mother spoke to my stepfather, bewildered, and asked, "Why do I still love him?"

*   *   *

It is April, and I am visiting my mother. We stand on her porch and look at what flowers are coming in this year, and those which remain stubborn. She leads me around the yard and then to the fence, points out a long row of daffodils. I ask if she planted those bulbs in September. She laughs. She sounds young. She gets down on one knee and touches a petal. "These," she says. "These have always been my favorite."

The Weight of Fire

Laconia, NH 1975

Smokers, my parents left matchbooks in almost every room of the house. I'd take a book I found lying around, hide it in my pocket, and go outside for the day. I'd then search out a quiet area on my street, huddle down between a paltry stand of trees, and pile up some dried leaves, bits of scrap paper, little black twigs, whatever, and tear off a match.

The sound of striking the head against the back of the book, that wet metallic clicking, made me feel powerful. And when the flame sprouted from the top of the match, that feeling deepened. I'd place the tip against a brown elm leaf or a crumpled milk carton, and as the fire slowly grew, eating at the bits of trash, I felt far away, detached, as if watching a TV show through someone else's eyes.

My parents started getting calls from everyone in the neighborhood that their "stuttering son" had started another fire. Adults would discover a loose pile smoldering behind the small brick school building, or maybe in Mrs. Chevalier's trashcan, white smoke climbing its invisible rope toward the empty, hot sky.

So one bright August morning, my dad showed up in front of our house straddling a ten speed. He didn't own a bike. On the back was a seat for a little kid. He found me out back playing with my older brother Brian, hitting rocks with a metal bat.

"Hey, Chris, wanna go for a ride?"

He showed me the bike and how I could fit into the seat. Brian wanted to know when he could get a ride on the bike, and my father told him soon, soon.

4

I was excited by the prospect of riding not only on a grownup bike, but also on one driven by my dad; I rarely had one-on-one time with him. My mom was more attentive, but she was young and just starting to discover her own sexuality—this, unfortunately, began to involve men besides my father.

The helmet I wore was too big for my head but I wore it anyway, the chin strap bulky against my neck. I loved the feeling of the warm air running past my face, the slight pump of tires churning against asphalt as my dad peddled.

Downtown was busy that day, cars slowly moving through lights and then stopping behind mirrored bumpers. A couple of young boys were fishing off a bridge next to the town's only hotel; they laughed in dirty t-shirts and teased each other. I turned and looked at the river escaping our city, going somewhere I could only dream of.

When we pulled up in front of the fire station, I was excited. We're visiting the fire trucks, I thought. Wow, what a surprise. I'd already spent a day visiting garbage trucks, a friend of my father's taking me to a dispatch center. He was the County Commissioner and had connections, and since he knew I loved garbage trucks, he was able to get me my own personal tour. My mom still has a glossy 8x10 photo of me being lifted up into the cab and looking quite shy. Afterward, I went to Dairy Queen and was allowed to have whatever I wanted. I started thinking which ice cream I'd get after this visit.

My dad stopped the bike near the side of the station and swung his right leg over the frame. He helped me out of the seat and helmet, leaned the bike against the gray wooden clapboards, and led me through the front door.

Several firemen were sitting around a folding table playing cards, dressed in regular clothes. Two men were quietly reading books and didn't even look up when we came in. I felt slightly deflated.

"Hey, I'm Rusty. I'm here with my boy to see The Chief."

Two guys got up from the table and said hello, that The Chief was upstairs expecting us. One of the younger men said he listened to my father on the radio. My dad always loved the recognition and chatted a bit before walking me up the steep flight of stairs.

The Chief was a plain man with average build, clean shaven face. He met us with a great smile and motioned for us to come in. The room was relatively empty save for some tightly made bunk beds and a large table in the middle of the room topped with a dollhouse. He squatted down to meet me face-to-face and introduced himself.

"So, you're our little fire starter, huh?" Chief Brown smiled.

I was confused, still wondering when I'd be able to climb into the cab of the hook and ladder, when I'd be able to place my helplessly small feet into the rubber boots and have my picture taken.

My father spoke with The Chief for a moment, hushed words that I could not make out, then said he was going downstairs. My dad smiled at me.

"Hey, after Chief Brown finishes up with you, I'll take you home, OK?" My dad then waved to me, which I thought was a little weird, and then made his way down the staircase.

"Come over here, will you Chris?" Chief Brown asked. He was still smiling and now standing next to the dollhouse.

I walked over and slowly climbed up on a small stool next to him. He removed the roof of the house and I was able to look down inside and see each individual room and small plastic figures of people.

"Does this look like your house, Chris?"

Thinking he wanted me to say yes I said yes.

"Where's your father here?"

I pointed to the figure which was clearly the dad. It wore blue overalls and held a lunch pail and was sitting in the living room, its plastic blue legs jutting straight out and toward a TV.

"And your mom?"

Again I pointed, this time at a female figure wearing an apron and standing over a stove and a little plastic roast chicken.

"Good, good." The Chief spoke in a soothing tone as he guided me.

"How about your brother, where is he?"

I pointed to a smaller figure smiling stiff atop a bed.

"And where are you, Chris?"

I looked and looked again but could not find a figure of me. My eyes darted back and forth as I searched for myself.

"I'm n-n-n-not there," I admitted.

"That's right you're not there. And do you know why you're not there, Chris?"

"N-n-n-no," I said, growing a little frightened.

The Chief put his nose real close to mine. I could see my face reflecting in his blue eyes.

"Because you're outside setting the house on fire, that's why. And your family is trapped inside and they're all going to die. Do you want them to die, Chris?"

I was horrified. "N-n-n-no!" I mewled. "I don't w-w-w-want them to all to g-g-g-get killed!"

"Well, that's what you're going to do, young man. You're going to kill your family." He picked up the figures and tried to make them walk out of the rooms they were in. Each time, he tipped them over and said the smoke got them, that they were now dead. I started to cry as I watched my family be subtracted one by one until all that remained was the unseen me, the ghostly me who orchestrated this massacre and was probably still lurking outside what remained of the home.

Afterward, my father biked me back home the way he brought me—in silence. There was no visiting the trucks, no pictures of me wearing oversized helmets. We did not go to Dairy Queen and I did not order the parfait, which was the ice cream I had decided on.

In two weeks I'd start first grade and stop lighting fires all together until my tenth birthday, made more memorable by the fact that I'd improperly extinguish a campfire and burn down the woods behind my house. "A hell of a set of candles," my father would say.

But after my visit with the Chief, I stayed outside until dinner and thought about all different types of fires: small, sputtering ones which don't do much of anything except sting your eyes with their cotton-colored smoke, and the giant ones which roar like strange creatures we'll never be able to fully understand or embrace. I had a matchbook in my dirty shorts pocket. On the inside cover was a phone number a man had written for my mother. Throughout the day I absently reached into my pocket and squeezed the matches, squeezed and released, the rhythm plain and steady, heart-like.

Call My Name

As a kid, I never went camping. Sure, there were one or two back-yard sleepovers with other boys in my church, and I'd once spent an unfortunate evening with my father and Brian in a neighbor's leaky cabin—my dad had been fighting with my mom again and sold the overnighter to us as a "bushwhacking adventure." But really, the closest I'd ever come to truly roughing it was watching Woody Woodpecker torment lumberjacks on our black-and-white television.

So I was shocked when my father announced one July that the family would spend the week camping on Cape Cod. On the way, we'd take a ferry over to Martha's Vineyard for the day to go biking. Sleeping in a tent under the stars sounded all right, but I was most excited about the ferry: I'd never been on a boat on the ocean before and was absolutely thrilled.

*   *   *

When we arrived to catch the ferry, I was deflated to learn we weren't riding on a pirate ship. In fact, the boat was downright ugly and shaped like a Styrofoam beach cooler. *Where are the masts?* I thought. *Couldn't they at least hang a plank off the side to threaten us?*

Following a sterile voyage filled with nothing but endless gray folds of water and a handful of trembling seagulls, we docked and were ushered down a gangway like doomed farm animals. I was overcome by the sheer number of people vacating the boat, pushing this way and that in their tennis shorts and reeking of Coppertone suntan lotion. On land, every store was selling something embroidered with an anchor, or else they displayed rows of driftwood lamps and lobster trap coffee tables. I couldn't see the beach and the place resembled any old town back in New Hampshire.

What a rip off.

My father eventually secured bicycles for us and said we would bike "the entire island"; since I had no idea how big Martha's Vineyard was I figured, well, there goes the summer.

Before we set out, my dad coaxed Brian and me over to a small dock, excitedly proclaiming that it was the very same spot that Sheriff Brody and Hooper dissected the tiger shark in the movie *Jaws*.

We looked down at the splintered planks waiting for something to happen. I hoped maybe I'd catch a glimpse of the bent license plate they pulled out of the shark's stomach; Brian reasoned it was probably in a trashcan nearby. I asked how they managed to get all the guts washed off the wood.

"Probably used a hose," my dad said.

*   *   *

Our ride was long and flat and hot. The people who drove past us in their air conditioned cars must have pitied us, or worse, laughed at an ill-prepared father leading his sweltering troupe on a bike ride to hell. Each time we stopped to take a break, (did we drink any water? I can't remember), my mother looked worse and worse, her face growing noticeably redder, her voice getting weaker.

When we arrived in the next town, we made a beeline for the first restaurant we found, disposing our bikes in a pile as if dumping medical waste. Huddled together around a dark, wood-paneled booth, we luxuriated in the cool air. My father ordered everyone jumbo iced teas. They were unsweetened, so Brian and I emptied packet after packet of sugar into the cups; the tea crunched with every sip.

"I just can't catch my breath, George," my mom said to my father. "I feel really sick."

"Drink your iced tea," he offered. "That will help. Come on, drink up."

Each time he told her to drink, I drank mine. None of us really talked, or joked. And no one mentioned the scenery of the island, as that would have only reminded us how far away from home we really were.

Back on the ferry I grew increasingly seasick. Brian and I played cards, Crazy Eights and War, but I could feel my stomach rolling in tandem with the ugly, cavernous ship. My mother seemed a little better, and she closed her eyes and rested her head on my father's shoulder. I could hear him humming softly into her ear.

*   *   *

When we backed up into our campsite, Brian and I were near busting with excitement. And once we piled out of the car and stretched our legs, I noticed the air had this silky aroma of wood smoke and pine trees, but bigger, cleaner.

My mom and dad pitched two tents as best they could: one for them and the other for us. My dad squeezed lighter fluid onto a pile of sticks and got a fire going. We noisily recounted the day over a dinner of hot dogs and beans.

Afterward, Brian grabbed a flashlight and we both wandered over to the lake. Several kids our age were hanging around the shore and laughing, throwing rocks in the air at bats or chucking branches into the blackened water. Two or three teenagers sat idling in a beige Rambler, windows down, Cheap Trick's "I Want You To Want Me" booming from their stereo. Those boys scared me.

But then I met Nathan.

Nathan had straight sandy-red hair and was from Southie. Every year, he said, his parents took him and his sister to this campground.

"You like c-c-coming here?" I stuttered slightly.

"Sure, I guess so. Can't complain."

"Yeah, that's good."

"Boston's too hot in the summer," he said.

"Do you hear a lot of sirens at night back home?" I asked, curious, as cities fascinated me.

"I guess so."

"I don't." I countered. "We live way up in the boonies in N-new Hampshire."

"Yeah? So why'd you come here?" Nathan asked. And I suddenly realized I had no idea at all.

*   *   *

During the day, our parents took us places normal families took their normal kids on vacation. We went to a little amusement park with its clunky, dubious rides and suspiciously hungover brake operators, and we also spent one afternoon at Plymouth Rock devouring peppermint stick ice cream cones and running the beach at low tide. The salty pinch of air made me feel elated. For once, I was like the kids I saw on TV, the ones who were so loved they didn't need to hear it repeated over and over to them like an apology.

By the third night, my parents' bickering began seeping back into our routine, so I spent my evenings with Nathan. We shared everything, even our own personal horror stories: Nathan and the vicious teasing he received for his red hair, me and my abusive third grade teacher from the year before. Sister Sally had finally crossed the line when she cold-cocked me in the face with a wooden paddle because I'd broken a plastic toy I'd won for reading the most books in class. That was not the last time I'd be knocked unconscious, but it certainly was the most upsetting.

Nathan loved that story, and I felt emboldened enough to move our friendship to the next level, so I told him about my church. New Christian Fellowship was Pentecostal, and every Sunday my family

and I witnessed at least one demonic possession and several occur-
rences of church leaders speaking in tongues. Our pastor believed
one of the most important tasks we could perform as Christians
was the recruitment of others, and with Nathan I suddenly understood I found my chance. I spoke casually about my church, and
just left the stuff out about the possessions: I didn't want to encourage any demons if they happened to be eavesdropping.

"Jesus loves you," I finally blurted. "Even though you don't
know it. He loves everybody."

"What? Why?" Nathan asked, waving away a firefly from his
face.

"Because he just does."

"Oh."

"And if you ask the Lord into your heart and accept him as your
savior, when you d-d-die, you will be in Heaven with him, like,
forever."

"Yeah?"

"Yeah." I paused briefly. "Will you accept Jesus into your heart?
Will you do that with me?" I could feel love spreading all throughout my body.

Nathan accepted my offer and let me pray for him. I felt so
proud of myself. And with both of us standing calmly there next
to that lake, I genuinely believed that I had just done something
packed with monumental goodness.

But really, what did I know.

Like the leaders in my church, and even my parents, I had
learned how to make quite an overture, but then didn't know how
to make any of it real: You Are Healed, You Are Saved, Our Family Will Be Just Fine.

Afterward, Nathan and I said goodnight and retreated to our
separate campsites. The next day my family packed up and headed
out, and I never saw Nathan again.

*   *   *

On our way back home, we spent the night at my grandfather's. I had become badly sunburned, and upon meeting me my aunt's new boyfriend he shook my hand and slapped me on the back several times. My skin exploded with pain. My eyes watered and I caught my breath. I excused myself and went out back to the woods so I could cry.

To get my mind off the pain, I thought about Nathan and our predestined meeting. I thought about my family, and I wondered what life would be like living with only one parent, something that day my mother said was going to happen if my father kept up with his quote-unquote bullshit. And then I thought about my sunburn, how painful it had become, and wished I knew how to make it all go away.

My mother started calling for me from the deck, and through the trees I could see her standing behind the waist-high railing about a hundred yards away. She was looking right at me but couldn't see me. And for a brief moment I liked that I was hidden but could see her so clearly in the setting light. I stood like that for a few seconds longer and felt immune to an adult world colored by disappointment and change. Then my mother raised her hands to her mouth and called my name again.

Possessed

There were strange hands on me. Some were small and cold, while others seemed large and rough and smelled of sawdust and cinnamon. The hands belonged to male church elders, who were encircling me in front of the entire congregation. Some of the men prayed aloud while others stood silent, their heads bowed. Mr. Daniels lead them. I knew Mr. Daniels because he had visited my house several times to pray with my dad. He was now squeezing my head and neck as I helplessly tried to make eye contact with my parents.

"Your son stutters because he is possessed by demons," Mr. Daniels informed my mother and father before the service began, as if he were reading from my medical chart. He'd leveled his eyes with my father's and said, "We must cast them from his body."

Other exorcisms were happening simultaneously throughout the chamber; I could hear wailing and the soft thuds of bodies hitting the floor. I called out for my father, and the men tightened their grips. My vision blurred, and I thought I was going to pass out. "Be gone," Mr. Daniels shouted. The other men hummed softly as one said, "Praise the Lord."

Then, just like that, it was over. Hands released their grip, and the men moved away like one body. Still dizzy, I reached out. One of the men grabbed my shirtsleeve to steady me, laughing softly. "Easy, Chris," he said. "It's okay."

Mr. Daniels guided me back to my family, his palm pressed gently between my shoulder blades. I stepped into the pew, embarrassed this had happened in front of so many people. My father smiled down at me and stroked my hair back while my mother shifted uncomfortably, saying nothing. I looked over at another group of church elders in a nearby corner, huddled around a man's twisted frame like hunters around a steaming buck.

Later, on the ride home, my father asked what I wanted for dinner, and I discovered I could answer him in complete sentences, my stuttering all but gone.

*   *   *

A month later—my mother pregnant with my sister Liz and due any day—I spent a week with a family who were also members of our church. I knew their son Jim from the church-run elementary school we both attended. Jim had recently had casts removed from both arms, which he'd broken after falling upside down from a jungle gym. In two months he would find himself back in the emergency room with shards of green glass embedded in his thighs and buttocks; after rolling down a grassy hill, he landed atop broken Coke bottles that were obscured by the tall grass. As doctors removed pieces of glass from his skin, the church elders met to discuss what Jim had done to displease the Lord so.

During my stay at Jim's house, I noticed how much time his family members spent together. They congregated at the kitchen table for meals and sang songs after dessert; they watched the *Muppet Show* together and laughed at the same parts. His mom was so attentive and kind to me I felt lonesome when I thought of my own mother.

My mom would nap daily with me wide awake beside her, and I'd listen to the slow draw of her breath as I planned my escape downstairs to watch *Creature Double Feature* on channel 56. Eventually she'd wake up from her afternoon nap, hair mussed, and I'd turn off the TV and help her prepare cube steak and French fries for dinner. Afterward, waiting for my father to return home, we'd dance to her Don McLean album, singing, "*The earth, the earth, the earth is my grave.*"

On my third night with the family, Jim's father thanked the Lord for having me be their guest. Everyone nodded and smiled around the dinner table, then held hands and recited a prayer, blessing the meal we were about to eat. At bedtime, I slipped into my fire-retardant pajamas and pulled back the covers of the makeshift bed set up next to Jim's. Then Jim got real close to me. I could feel his right arm firm against my left. His breathing quickened.

"Do you want to feel good?" he asked.

As he wrapped his hand around my small penis, I never knew I had a choice.

Afterward, Jim crawled into his bed without a word and fell asleep. I felt alien and detached in the darkness, still sitting on the edge of my bed.

*   *   *

We went to school the next morning, and I found out that my mother had had a C-section, and my mother and new sister would be in the hospital for a few more days. I was excitedly telling this to my friend Danny when my second-grade teacher slapped me on the back of the head and ordered me to continue coloring in my Bible workbook. I lowered my head and pressed my crayon to a picture of a camel and the betrayed Joseph, his treacherous brothers looming in the background.

That night, Jim was more demanding. He had me pull my pajamas down to my ankles, and we rubbed our penises together like starting a fire. All the while, it seemed that I was falling, that the world was turning to dust beneath my feet. I closed my eyes and tried to think about home. I conjured up memories of Saturday mornings watching cartoons with my father. He'd place his hand on my neck and rest it there, and I'd be happy to feel its weight. *I'm going home soon*, I thought, and then Jim brought me back, gripping my shoulder to steady himself.

*   *   *

The first night back home, I was wakened by thick screams. My brother Brian and I crept to the stairs and peeked between the banisters. A man we knew from church lay on the hardwood floor, sputtering and convulsing, his lips shiny with spit and his eyes rolled back in his head. My father and other men closed in on him, shouting incantations, their arms extended as if pushing at a great invisible force. They rebuked the evil spirit and demanded it leave his body. The man screamed louder while Brian and I looked on, frozen by the need to watch, paralyzed by our fear of leaving.

The next day, my father asked me to go into the bathroom with him. Usually this meant a swift and merciless spanking, but I noticed he wasn't gripping a hairbrush or spatula as I lagged behind. He closed the door, sighed, and ran his arthritic hand down his thick, reddish beard. My father looked more tired than I'd ever seen him.

"You know why we're talking, don't you, Chris?"

"No," I offered. The small window behind his head framed the sun and made my father's hair look like it was on fire.

"I spoke with Jim's parents."

I stared at him blankly, not sure what more he would say.

"Jim told his folks what you made him do. Chris, what you did was a sin."

"Oh."

"You see, in situations like this, the Lord is liable to take his hand off you for a while and allow bad things to happen to you. Do you understand?"

"Yes."

My dad stared at me. He seemed unsure of what to say next.

"I don't want to talk about this again, OK? Now, go outside and play."

Down the street I found Brian on a neighbor's bike, driving over a makeshift jump and popping wheelies in the dust. As I watched, I thought about what my dad said. *He's right*, I thought. *It's all my fault.*

*   *   *

My parents stayed with the church for a few more years, then we moved to another town. One night soon afterward, they told us over bowls of spaghetti that they were getting divorced. Even so, we went back to the church for a couple of Sundays; my father drove us the hour and a half in our green Volare station wagon with the windows up, my mom's perfume choking us. But after some of the church elders told my mother that she should stay married to my father, sell the new house, and move back to the area, my mother knew she could never come back. Infuriated by her stubbornness, Mr. Daniels told her, "Well, it's a long drive back, Pat. Let's hope the Lord doesn't decide to have your brakes go out."

As the weeks of divorce proceedings dragged on, my father grew increasingly agitated, shaking his fist and exalting the Lord as he walked through each room of the new house. He later told Brian and me that the house was "unclean," that demons hid in every corner.

I sat up most nights and listened for these demons, wondering what they looked like and if I could hear their claws scuttling across the floor. In the dark, I became convinced that the pipes banging in the cellar were a whole legion of them, teeth-gnashing and horrible, waiting to devour me.

After about a week of this, each night progressively worse, I woke up feeling sick, having wet the bed the night before. I don't remember much, but do recall walking around the house physically shaking and mumbling. When my father couldn't snap me out of my stupor, he took me back to my room, sat me on his lap, and began to pray. As he did, I realized that I was breathing in short, ragged gasps. I also realized that my father was saying things like, *leave his body* and *release him.* That's when I understood that he was praying for me because he believed that I was possessed, that my soul was engulfed by a dark and dreadful thing.

I was beginning to wonder if I was in fact filled with demons when my father raised his voice and commanded the spirits to leave me in the name of God. At that point, my own voice separated from my body, as if someone had turned up the volume in my chest and I had no control. My throat released a horrifying scream, rasped and ugly, and I knew that it was not my voice. After all these years of watching people flail about in my church, writhing and foaming into a crushed heap, at last it was happening to me.

My monstrous scream surprised and terrified me so much that I lurched toward my father's body and dug my fingers into his soft flannel shirt. I felt weak and weightless across his legs, and I began sobbing. My father held me close and assured me that I was okay. The Lord had saved me, he said, and the next breath I'd take would again be my own. It was one of the last times my father and I would hold each other so close.

The final week he lived with us, my father completely secluded himself. He had taken a part-time job at a pizza shop in town, and when he came home from work, he would go into his room without a word and lock the door. Brian and I saw him only when he emerged for more beer. I wondered if he was writing, or maybe drawing cartoons like he did when I was younger. He had always told my mother that he had the "soul of an artist" and, because of that, found it impossible to perform menial tasks around the house or work at a job that required extended commitment or responsibility.

Months later Brian and I searched our father's old room. Instead of finding stories or drawings, however, all we discovered were a couple of audio cassettes stuffed into a shoe box. Dates were scribbled across each cassette; Dad had made the bulk of the recordings during the last week he was home. We sat at the kitchen table, slid one of the tapes into our mother's cassette recorder, and pressed PLAY.

At first it sounded like our father was telling the story of King Arthur, but eventually my brother and I realized he was trying to imagine a better life for himself. I was confused by how happy he sounded. He said if he had lived in a different time, he'd like to have a brigade of long bowmen at his disposal versus crossbowmen, or perhaps a magnificent, shimmering troop of armored knights to protect him if he were the feared yet benevolent king of a medieval fiefdom. My brother and I listened for a couple of hours, then finally gave up and stopped the tape.

After the divorce was finalized, my father moved into an all-male boardinghouse in town. Among other things, he took the black-and-white TV he'd kept on the back porch, which had been his retreat when he and my mother were fighting. One night Brian and I went to visit him at the boardinghouse and watch a Celtics game on TV. We looked on as Celtics star Larry Bird performed athletic feats we could only dream of. "God, he's good," Dad said. Brian and I agreed, nodding silently as we watched Bird run up and down the court, putting the other team to shame. "When's your mother coming to get you?" he asked.

"You already asked that," I said.

As my father rummaged for more beef jerky in an empty plastic bag, I gazed at the TV and knew I would never come back to this place with its lonely wooden hallways, its strange shadows, its recently divorced fathers living under one sad roof.

Toward the end of the basketball game, we heard a car horn outside. Brian and I peered out the third-floor window and saw my mom's station wagon idling in the street. We said goodbye to our father. As I embraced him, I could hear small noises in his throat as if he were trying to speak. I hugged him tighter, and pressed my ear to his chest.

Unforgivable

The richest members of our old church owned a racetrack, and as a favor to my father one summer they hired Brian and me to help sell programs. And as we schlepped the glossy magazines back and forth in front of bleachers teeming with be-leathered motorcycle enthusiasts, rednecks, and ZZ Top look-alikes, I realized I had never been so scared in all my life.

It was the infamous Motorcycle Weekend, and as the sun pounded us and the Ducati motorcycles whined around the track, my brother and I each lifted a magazine meekly above our heads and mouthed the word "program" for any lip readers in attendance. The haze of gas and oil created its own weather system, the air both noxious and sweet.

To get our attention, a biker would jam a tattooed arm into the sky, and then either my brother or I climbed the shiny aluminum planks to receive our customer. Surprisingly, the gentlemen always said "Thank you" and "Please," and never tried to shortchange us, patiently waiting as we counted out the bills from our aprons, tens and twenties sticking out all over the place and sometimes falling to the ground.

"Um, son, you seem to be losing a bit of your money there," one man said who sported a Fu Manchu mustache and t-shirt that pictured a bride and groom above the words "Game Over." "No, no, you're giving me back too much change, boy," said another, his black vest festooned in buttons showcasing assault rifles nestled between an assortment of naked breasts. Looking back, I think they were so honest with my brother and me because we were painfully young and too easy a target. I mean, where's the honor in rolling a couple of skinny and nervous-looking white boys who reeked of innocence and decent bedtimes?

When we sold our lot, we made our way back to a little trailer near the park entrance, past the beer booths and a line of port-a-potties that were more like cholera outbreaks in training, and dumped our cash in big piles on the trailer floor. My brother and I would then grab a new stack of magazines and enough cash to make change, and repeat the process all over again.

During our third trip back to the trailer Brian showed me a $20 bill he had stashed in his pocket. "Who cares," he said. "It's not like anybody's counting."

*   *   *

My mother and father had been divorced for about a year by this point, and my father had finally left the boardinghouse and moved in with his own mom back in Laconia. My mom was trying to raise four kids on a secretary's salary while simultaneously paying off a new mortgage and my father's lingering debts. We hadn't had hot water that past winter, or even oil heat; to save money, my mom had bought two cords of unseasoned wood. In fact, when the guy dropped it off in our driveway, he dumped a pile of logs that had been clearly sitting out in the elements for weeks; crusted in sleet and snow, the wood was as frozen as the icicles hanging from our roof. Brian and I were relegated to "digging duty" as we pawed through the snowy heap and collected the best-looking specimens to stand next to the woodstove to dry. I can still hear the sound of all that wood sizzling as the ice melted into large puddles on the floor and my younger brother Josh and sister Liz asked for another blanket while eating cinnamon toast on the couch.

On one occasion, my mom brought home a large plastic bag filled with uncooked Kentucky Fried Chicken. We had no idea that my mom knew someone who snuck a bagful out of the restaurant to stash behind a dumpster for her to pick up after work.

We rarely saw our dad by this point. And his absence probably contributed in making him an even more mythical, god-like figure than he already was to us. When my dad wasn't around, I could imagine him doing great things, or better yet, imagine that he was terribly unhappy without us, and sorry for going away. I had one daydream in particular where I pictured him standing in my bedroom doorway, keys in his hand, asking if I wanted to go with him to Hampton Beach to play video games and get some fried dough. I came out of the reverie before I could say yes.

*   *   *

By summertime, my dad announced we'd spend a week with him. He sweetened the deal by saying he got Brian and me a job at the track. *At last*, I thought. *I finally get to do something dangerous.*

The day he came to pick us up, my dad drove Grampa's old Cadillac. Long, red, and shark-like, the car had air conditioning powerful enough to run a city morgue. As we drove away, my mom waved from the picture window, cigarette in her hand.

"Is this Grampa's car?" I asked, marveling at all the space and enjoying the cool leather seats. Comparatively, our station wagon smelled like yogurt and gasoline.

"Yep," my father said. "I didn't think he would mind." Grampa had died of a heart attack two years previous, and the Cadillac had been just sitting in his garage.

My grandmother lived in a big house with an even bigger back yard, and to have so much space was liberating. After unpacking we decided to haul the croquet set out of the garage and smack the brightly colored balls throughout the yard, aiming for each other's ankles.

We explored the creepy garage. One wall was lined with old New Hampshire license plates; seeing the words "Live Free or Die" up and down in little aluminum rows made me feel terrified. I wondered if Grampa's ghost was hidden behind the dust and broken umbrellas stacked in the rear of the garage. Brian then accidentally broke a window by swinging a golf club around like a Musketeer, and we made a hasty retreat.

That night, after everyone went to bed, Brian and I snuck into the living room to watch HBO—our TV back home got six channels. We anxiously huddled before the TV's blue glow.

"What's this?" Brian asked, and the words on the screen said *The Exorcist.*

Two hours later, Brian and I lay sweating in the dark, staring up at what we hoped was only the ceiling.

"Hey, do you think all that stuff in the movie happened?" I asked Brian. It was almost three in the morning.

"Sure it happened. Probably happens all the time."

"Really?"

"That movie was based on real people," he said. "Real events."

We were then quiet for a bit.

"What was that?" I asked.

"What?"

"That sound."

"Try to hold your breath," Brian suggested. "They won't know you're here if they can't hear you breathe."

*   *   *

The next morning was our first day at the track, and after Brian's revelation, we had pocketed over $80 each by mid-afternoon. We felt absolutely alive and in charge. In fact, that night, we treated everyone to dinner at the Tamarack Drive-in, feasting on clam boats, hot dogs, and French fries. We told our dad the bikers had been generous with their tips. After dinner, we barreled over to

Funspot and gorged on video games, the change machine emptying like a loose Vegas slot as Brian and I slid in one five dollar bill after another. We were better than rich, we thought. We were famous.

The next day at the racetrack, Brian and I took more money, high on the simplicity of it all, our hands electric as we folded one twenty after another into our dirty jeans front pockets. We found our voices that day, shouting out the word *Programs!* with such poise that the bikers in the stands grew anxious with our bravado, and changed their demeanor. Nobody likes a confident kid hawking over-priced magazines to hungover bikers in the middle of the heat.

Nobody.

*   *   *

After the week finally passed and our father dropped us off back home, Brian and I went to our room to secretly discuss how we'd spend our money. After a final tally, we hauled in about $300 each. I started thinking about all kinds of things I wanted to buy: BB guns, fireworks, maybe an Atari 2600 so we could play Pac-Man. I couldn't believe our good fortune. I almost thanked God, but then, you know, realized I'd probably burn in hell if I did.

Right when I was going to mention the Atari to Brian, my mom walked in our room and asked again if we had fun and if we did anything "out of the ordinary." *Damn it*, I thought. *We're caught.*

"No," I offered. "You know, just hung out and stuff. Watched TV."

"Really? Didn't do anything…different?" She sounded a bit like she was pleading, and her voice cracked, and I now felt less scared and just more confused.

I looked at Brian. "Ummm…nope," I said.

That's when I noticed my mother was shaking a little bit.

"You mean to tell me that you two big spenders didn't think it's 'fun' or 'different' to take everyone out to eat the other night?"

I was completely baffled until I remembered the Tamarack Drive-In and how Brian and I sprang for the meal.

"Your father said he had a *great* time out at dinner! Did *you* have a good time? Huh?"

"I, I guess so, mom," said Brian.

"What about me!" my mother suddenly yelled, and Brian and I flinched. "You've never taken me out anywhere! All these things I do, how hard I work. What about something like this for me and not some man that doesn't even love you enough to call you on your birthday!"

"Wait mom, we were gonna do this for you too," I lied.

"Oh, you're so full of shit!" she yelled.

"Well, excuse us for not knowing that love was something we had to buy from you!" Brian countered.

My mother's eyes narrowed. "It has nothing to do with that. How dare you!"

The three of us just stood there, unaware of the next move.

"I hope you enjoy all your money and I'm so glad you were able to spend such quality time with your...your...*father!*" She then quickly left and went into her bedroom, slamming the door behind.

Brian and I were thunderstruck. In awe, actually. Where was it written that spending money on our dad meant we didn't love her? I mean, didn't she know that we loved her most of all?

*   *   *

Any plans Brian and I had of buying up the world with our windfall faded very quickly: we were ruined by greed. When we returned from a downtown shopping adventure the next day with a new boom box, over a dozen albums, Ocean Pacific t-shirts, several bags of candy, and the promise to go back the following day to get what we couldn't fit into our arms the first time around, my mom knew.

When she questioned Brian and me one at a time in the bathroom, we caved. We didn't even put up a fight when she asked how we managed to buy as much as we did. The math didn't make sense, she said. But the weird thing was, my mom wasn't as angry as I had expected her to be. She just seemed... tired. Like she understood how we could be so easily seduced by all those piles of cash and wished she could just look the other way, but knew that would be unforgivable.

When my mom took the remainder of our money and mailed it back to the owners of the track, along with a long letter from both Brian and me asking for mercy, they responded by sending us a very chipper note saying that we shouldn't worry about it. They even invited us to work at the track next year. We were floored. How, in the midst of such blatant disregard for trust and respect, could they respond by acting so kind?

How could they possibly forgive us for all that we had done?

Friction

The day after my sixteenth birthday, I noticed a small, sharp thing on my bedroom floor. I picked it up as if I'd been looking for it my whole life. It could have been metal. Or a piece of glass. I don't remember. But I do remember what it wasn't. It certainly wasn't a knife, or a razor. Razors came later, and at that point holding a tool whose only job was to cut would have been too obvious, and my actions telegraphed not just to the world, but to me. The item had to be as ambiguous as my intentions. If someone walked into my bedroom as I sat on the edge of my mattress, slicing back and forth across my bare thighs and asked me what the hell was I doing, I could look up at them, holding this bent piece of anonymous whatever, and smile. *Oh, this old thing? Why it's nothing at all.*

*   *   *

I loved bands like Fear, 7Seconds, Circle Jerks, Black Flag. Punk rock allowed me the release that living in a small town didn't. When David pressed play on his tape deck in his parked car, and the Dead Kennedys shouted about Nazi punks and how they should fuck off. I grabbed Jules by his leather jacket and spun him around in the field we were drinking in. We spun faster. It was exhilarating not knowing how it would end. Tim passed a joint to Steph. Bea said 5 Balls Of Power were playing in Kittery next week. Scooter said he was getting some acid from his friend in California. David opened the car doors so we all could hear the music better. Finally my spinning slowed and Jules held onto my shirt, laughing. I laughed too, kicking at the weeds and asking for another beer. No one could touch us. We were a million miles away from parents and cops. My mother's black eyeliner overran, stinging. Steph said next week his parents were out of town, party at his place.

Later, Jack showed me the burn marks he made on his skin, a single repeating welt across his bare shoulder.

"You just heat the tip of a lighter red hot," he said.

*   *   *

There was this older punk from Arizona who now lived in Portsmouth. Steph spoke of him with a kind of reverence.

"At this party, he took off his shirt," Steph said. "And then he dragged a razor straight across his chest. From shoulder to shoulder."

"Seriously," I said. "Holy shit."

"Fucking badass," Steph said.

*   *   *

Steph's party was packed. Ed showed up late and held two beers, saying he needed to catch up. My sometimes girlfriend Laura was there, dressed like a fucking preppy. But she was beautiful, and I didn't really know how to talk to her.

Steph then raised his hand at me across the dining room and glinted his prize: a fresh razor between his fingers. He smiled.

Upstairs in his room we took a few hesitant swipes, small scratches high up on the shoulder, places our t-shirts would cover. A few kids hung around and gaped, duly impressed. I peppered the razor down the length of my right arm, and then made three parallel lines from elbow to wrist.

"Duuuuude," Ed said.

Laura watched me closely. "I don't like razors," she said, and left the room.

Good, I thought. Fuck you.

I then pushed the razor deep into my left arm. Pulled. It opened like a baby's mouth.

At first, the blood was shy. Then it overran everything. I cut a tic tac toe board and felt no pain.

I win, I thought.

*   *   *

I woke up on Steph's bed, my left arm stuck to the sheet. It was Saturday and my father was coming to pick me and my siblings up for the weekend. I washed my arm but it started bleeding again. I wrapped the wound in toilet paper and pulled both sleeves down.

*   *   *

The whole weekend I spent trying to hide what I'd done. My dad and his new wife were kind, tried to offer fun things for all of us to do. That night we made Buffalo wings. I watched as the chicken skin bubbled and contracted in the hot oil. My brother stirred the sauce on the stove, a slurry of bright red.

"Who's hungry?" my dad said.

I kept checking my sleeves to make sure they didn't slide up.

*   *   *

In school on Monday, I showed Steph my arm and he laughed with me, said I was crazy. I know, I said. I know. We talked about the weekend, maybe going to Boston.

"Who's playing?" I asked.

"Gang Green," Steph said.

"Okay. I'll see what I can do. I'm probably grounded."

We laughed at this. My running joke: I was always grounded.

"See you at lunch," I said.

"See you."

I stood at my locker for an extra second, touched my sleeve, the ache beneath. I felt so lonely I wanted to fall to my knees.

"Hey, you're late, you're late," Mr. Delcroix said, stepping from the language lab.

I looked at him. He had made it his personal mission to get David expelled. It worked.

"Not yet," I said, moving in the other direction.

"You're on my hit list, Locke," he called.

I hurried down the hallway, through the science wing and its corny posters about planets and the universe and how fun it is to learn. I imagined for a second what it would feel like to float in space, untethered; to slip past all those things that could hurt you.

Stagedive

I believed it was love, so I shimmied out the bedroom window, fell into my parents' rhododendrons, and then scrambled up the dirt road and into the back of David's waiting Gran Torino. We were going to a show in Kittery.

More importantly, Juliana was also in Kittery. In Spanish class on Friday she told me: "*Me gusta Cristobal.*"

But I'd been caught smoking hash the week before and was still grounded. So I begged. I pleaded—seriously, I pleaded—I told my mom about Juliana and that this would be our first date.

My mom stared into my eyes and frowned.

"No," she said.

When we got to Kittery, the bands were between acts and Juliana was already in the alley chugging beers. David and the others went inside as I quickly introduced my shivering body to Juliana's in the narrow darkness. We shared the rest of her Budweiser. Juliana's mouth found my mine as the next band started to warm up. We pushed against the brick wall. The grimy window above our heads began chattering with reverb and dust fell into her hair and across my hand.

Later, show over and driving home, the dashboard clock glowed 1:10 a.m. I was dizzy with vodka and the spent exhaust of some homegrown I smoked out of a Mountain Dew can. The Circle Jerks pounded from Dan's tape deck, Sean and Tom yelling along, windows down: *Wild in the streets! Running! Running! Wild in the streets!* Their voices slipped harmlessly between all the vacant sidewalks and quiet homes lining our way.

The veracity of going AWOL was growing more palpable by the minute; I had never done anything like it before and was starting to panic. I tried to convince myself that my mother and stepfather would never check on me again before going to bed themselves and that for all they knew I was cozied up in my room dreaming the dreams of good sons.

I walked my dirt driveway as quietly as I could, careful not to kick any stones. I snuck behind the house, peered up at my parents' window. No lights.

I pushed open the cellar door, eased into the darkness, and felt my way across the cement. When I got to the stairs, I took off my Converse All-Stars, placed them in my hand, and ghosted up to the main door, the last threshold to cross.

I stood there for several seconds and listened: not a sound. I turned the knob slowly and pushed with the gentlest urging. Everywhere was dark. I sighed. I stepped into the kitchen.

Loud clamoring burst from my parents' bedroom, and their door boomed open. And as my mother stormed across the hardwood floor in her nightgown, murder in her voice, I thought how wonderful it would be to live with Juliana in Kittery, and how every night she could stagedive into my waiting arms, and that I would lift her up, hold her beautifully above the others.

Another Life

My mother and I were going to murder each other if I didn't move out. It'd been a year since I graduated high school, and we could barely say two words to each other. However, standing on the front porch hugging her and my stepfather after I packed, I cried. Sobbed, actually. I knew nothing could ever be the same. And even if someday I did return, if I flamed out gloriously and crawled back humiliated and broken, I knew I was still gone for good.

My girlfriend's Toyota Tercel was packed tight with the essentials: clothes I'd lumped into trash bags; my extensive collection of punk albums and colored vinyl (which would later all be stolen); a journal I'd never written in given to me by my sister; an "Old Ghosts" skateboard (also soon stolen); a 13-inch black-and-white TV; and a smudged baseball signed by every member of the 1978 Red Sox—in a fit of lamentable buffoonery, I added my own signature in blue ink when I was nine.

The weather that day was fittingly overcast. Early November. I looked back as I drove up the hill, my parents waving from the steps. I wiped my eyes and tried to avoid potholes, the Tercel's suspension unforgiving.

I arrived at my girlfriend's place on the seacoast and was shown my room: Evelyn was eighteen and lived with her mom in a Victorian sprawl shaded by a legion of doting maple trees. Her mom had been divorced for years and clearly liked me; when she'd take Evelyn and me out to dinner, she'd smile across the table and say things like: "Oh, Chris, in thirty years you're going to be such looker." I was like, *Wait, what's wrong with me now?* I didn't realize how deep her affection ran. She once burst through the front door as Evelyn and I were having sex on the couch, but she walked in with her back turned, pretending to be calling the cat until Evelyn and I could disentangle and snap our trunks back up, out of breath and fumbling with the TV remote.

Besides that, for the first month at least, things seemed good: I got a job as a waiter at a fancy breakfast joint in the center of town. At night, Evelyn and I would meet up with our friends Brianna and Karen and go driving around, smoking clove cigarettes and cranking New Order on the tape deck. We'd roll up to out-of-the-way convenience stores and ask frustrated middle-aged men to buy us beer. Later, creeping about the cemetery in Portsmouth we'd tell ghost stories while ducking behind carved angels resplendent with moss. I'd chug my fourth or fifth Coors Light until my head percolated. And at some point I'd look up at the black and mottled sky and literally breathe a sigh of relief that I didn't need to hurry home because I was breaking curfew again, setting the stage for another midnight confrontation with my mother.

But in March everything changed. Evelyn had a breakdown and was taken to the hospital by ambulance; Evelyn had been on and off different antidepressants for years, and always seemed to vacillate somewhere between radiant joy and the darkest hollows. But I loved her, or thought I did, and I would just wait for her to come back around—which she always would—and everything again was normal.

This time was different. I was eating dinner with Evelyn and her mother at the dining room table when Evelyn abruptly excused herself and went upstairs. We heard her yelling a few minutes later. I found Evelyn hiding under her bed in tears, covering her face. As I reached for her, trying to console her and saying her name gently, she yelled "No!" over and over, swiping at my hand. Finally, her mother called 911 and she was removed from the house. I could only look on helplessly as the ambulance doors whumped closed.

After visiting Evelyn in the hospital almost every day for two weeks, I was met by her mother on the porch in her bathrobe. She was waiting for me. Wild-eyed, she pointed and said things like "You did this to her! This is your fault! You caused all of Evelyn's... suffering!" She spit that last word out at me. *Suffering.* And I was dumbfounded, almost furious, because I didn't understand at the time that some parents who lose their children will grasp at anything to keep themselves from going under too.

I threw Evelyn's car keys on the porch and walked away. Big hero. *Now what,* I thought.

I went to my one-room apartment a couple of blocks away; staying at Evelyn's had always been just a stopgap until I found my own place. Apparently, I found it at a boarding house with five other dudes on Ham Street. We all shared a bathroom down the hall next to a toaster oven. We paid the same $60 per week, utilities included, for single rooms that came furnished with a dresser, desk, and double bed.

I sat on the edge of my mattress and finished some Thai weed my buddy Scott had gifted me. I blew the smoke out the window and tried to think of a plan. All I could think about were hot meals and a bed that didn't smell like someone else's perspiration. I put Morrissey's new album on and laid back down, reading the lyric sheet. Morrissey crooned along to the words as I read them. He sang about hiding on promenades, marking his confessions on the back of a postcard, dearly wishing to be elsewhere.

I played the album over and over. Partly because I believed Morrissey sang my truths, but mostly because I didn't own anything else; my albums got snatched off the porch as I was moving in a month prior.

I turned back to the open window and felt the first real spring day give way to evening and its strange perfumes, the soft patter of cars knocking up and down the street as their headlights blinded the back fence and a few withered snowbanks. I didn't know what I wanted to do, but I knew it wasn't this. The idea of college was still a mystery. I wanted to go home but I didn't know where home was.

I stood up and flipped the album over. I was worried about Evelyn. Almost every time I had driven up to the hospital, I saw figures silhouetted in the windows staring down at me. After I'd park the car and lock the door, I'd look back up and think those people probably hoped I was someone they knew; someone who once loved them in another life.

How It Began Before It Ended

It was two a.m. Billy's Jetta was parked on the curb and I sat in passenger seat, top down. I felt vulnerable in the dark, uneasy with the city's brick tenements and low sound. Directly overhead, a streetlight flickered like a dying brain. It was warm and I was dressed in shorts, a black t-shirt. I thought about my wife Lisa and daughter Grace asleep at home and shifted my weight; my thighs stuck to the leather seats.

I replayed the evening in my head: After dinner, I finished grading my students' papers on Thoreau's theory of needs vs. wants and reread five pages of Marquez's *100 Years of Solitude* for another class. I changed Grace's diaper and handed her off to Lisa, kissing them both and saying I'd be back by 11:00 at the latest. I went to my Saab, did four bumps of coke off the house key, inhaled deeply, and squeezed my eyes shut until the stinging passed.

When I arrived at a party in town, I had some whiskey, a little more coke, and another whiskey. Then a white kid with dread-locks got angry because all the tiki torches outside made the lawn resemble a landing strip, burning a symmetrical pattern that made him furious somehow. He pulled them out of the ground, one at a time, and threw them sputtering into the pool. A glass table followed.

That's when Billy showed up, and what we both wanted was only twelve minutes away. We would look for Psychs again. My heart raced. On the way, we drank beer from red plastic cups and talked about our students; we worked at the same school. The new batch of kids seemed more docile, Billy said. I mentioned how much I liked the new boy from Jersey and all his mad energy, the love for Emerson he professed in my English class. A quarter of the kids we worked with were at the school for drug abuse, the others had social/emotional issues, learning disabilities, or a combination of all three. We were viewed as one of the finest therapeutic boarding schools in the country. We offered group counseling three days a week. Just the day before, I sat across from a girl and spoke in a soft tone as she held her head in her hands and sobbed. Her long red hair fell around her wrists like spun fire. "I can't believe I'm here," she choked. I know, I said. I know.

At graduations, I was always a favorite to speak on behalf of a graduating student. For example, I discussed how hard it'd been for _____, that he'd overcome major trauma. Back home, he saw someone get tied to a tree and then set on fire for not paying a drug dealer. The sound of that boy screaming woke him up every night. This young man learned, I said, to love his family, and himself, again. At the end of the speech, as with all my speeches, I cried. The student cried. His family and the other well-dressed families cried. "You can do this," I said. We embraced and then, bravely, he went back into the world.

We found Psychs where we did last time, hanging out in front of the small, withered park downtown. He wore a red Chicago Bulls jersey, cargo shorts and was sitting indifferently atop a cement ledge. I don't think he remembered us. As we drove him to the place, Billy asked if I could front the money for the heroin. I said I didn't have the money, thought he had it.

"What," Psychs said from the back. "You ain't got the fuckin' money?"

"No, no, we'll get it," I promised. "Where's that ATM around here?"

The last time we did this, which was also the first night we ever met Psychs, we managed to do the same exact thing: try to score heroin without remembering to bring any cash. "It'd be a bad night to get knifed," Psychs said then, and I believed him, picturing a cartoon Arabian sword pushed through the seats and into our backs, Psychs rolling our stupid corpses out onto the curb. "Stay in the suburbs," he'd say as he drove off in the Jetta.

This time, after collecting a hundred dollars from the ATM, we pulled up in front of the apartment and Billy turned to Psychs. "Don't give us any of that white boy shit," he said. "We want the normal dime bags, ten of them."

"Hey, don't fucking talk to me," Psychs said. "Just give me the money." He took the five twenties, quickly exited and crossed the dark street, disappearing like a spider down a flower's throat. I was starting to feel hung over and the coke had worn off.

Silently, Billy and I waited ten minutes.

"That motherfucker better not screw us," Billy said. A car moved softly down a cross street, left no evidence that it had ever been there.

"I'm going in."

"In? In where," I asked.

"Don't worry, I'm just gonna see if he's in the stairwell or something."

He left and I sat in the car alone.

I kept waiting for the police to roll up behind me with their spotlight blinding the mirror, their careful approach to my door as they asked to see my hands.

Someone came out of the building and walked with great purpose towards the car.

Billy opened the door and hopped in. "Hold these," he ordered. I looked at my hands and counted ten small plastic bags. He started the Jetta and we drove off.

"I already had a taste," he said, sliding the vehicle smoothly into third gear. "It's fucking amazing."

And I believed him because what other choice did I have?

The Night Faerie

Jim took the gun out of his waistband and put it in my hand.

Turning its weight over carefully, I thought the pistol looked like the kind James Bond favored when he was busy plugging Russians. The fluorescent lights of the hospital made the barrel seem grayer, its scratches more prominent. I handed the gun back to Jim, my fingertips oily.

"Yep, you could shoot that fucking thing. Right in the head," Jim said.

"Yeah. I don't know."

"Or I could." Jim offered.

"Put it away," I said, glancing over my shoulder. An IV machine in the next room started beeping like an alarm. An old woman muttered "Goddamnit," and the machine went silent.

"Just something to think about." Jim tucked the weapon back into his waistband.

I was starting to feel radiant; the five Percocet I'd recently swallowed were kicking in, and I could feel their slow, warm crawl up and through my chest, my head, and even my hair. It was almost possible to believe that my four-year-old daughter Sophie was not lying asleep and bandaged behind me, her face and neck badly damaged.

"Did you bring those Valium?" I asked, and Jim furrowed his brow, his hand at last slipping into his coat front pocket.

*　　*　　*

43

We couldn't have ordered better weather for the picnic: it was late afternoon, the August sun starting its slow descent and blessing everything it touched with a buttery gold. We were in the Berkshires, Lisa and I having just taken jobs as teachers at a small boarding school. The campus included acres and acres of deep rolling hills and swaying fields. Green found ways to reproduce itself everywhere. Classes were still a few weeks off and we had nothing but time. A couple of teachers—new to the school, just like us—invited me and my wife and daughters to a picnic across the street. How could we say no?

I packed a store-bought roast chicken, a bottle of icy Spanish white wine. Lisa made broccoli salad. When we stepped outside our two daughters instinctively ran as if on a prison break; Grace tried to perfect back handsprings while Sophie did her best to mimic her. Lisa slipped her hand into mine as we smiled and continued on, offering words of encouragement to both. I liked how Lisa's arm felt against mine as we walked. Before we left, I took a few Percocet on an empty stomach. I had bought twenty-five pills from Jim the night before and felt relieved that I now had enough to get me through the week.

We stopped in the middle of a mown field where the others had already gathered. Jack, the new theatre director and music teacher, spread a baby blue blanket out across the grass. His soon-to-be ex-wife smiled radiantly beside him, sipping lemonade from a tall glass filled with raspberries. Pete, a recent PhD recipient in organic chemistry, was talking about his latest trip to Turkey and how it felt so strange and invigorating to hear the call to prayer when he was dozing in his fleabag hotel. "It's the first time I felt truly alien," he said, smiling at us through his reddish beard. Nearby, a giant maple cast an impressive visage, and it even had a long rope swing hanging from one of its branches; the girls immediately attached themselves to its loose rocking.

We bantered; we laughed and ate until all we could do was pick crumbs from the blanket. The chicken sank into its pile of bones.

A yellow bobolink skirted the top of high grass, its voice like a soft bubbling cauldron.

Then Victor arrived with his wife and his dog.

Victor taught Ancient History. He was the kind of sad educator who believed in the tidy evisceration of creative thought via endless lecture and the Gestapo-like memorization of date upon tiresome date. If a student nodded off in class, Victor resorted to chucking dry erase markers at head level.

There was a slight chill in the air; the pills had worn off and I was feeling tired and clumsy. Lisa was trying to wrangle the girls, saying we had to get going. We repacked all our plastics into a canvas bag; the empty wine bottle sat naked on the grass.

Sophie loved animals. All her favorite books were about horses, cats, and dogs. We would sometimes go to Pet Smart and ask to see the cats. Sophie would look down at them and speak softly as she gently stroked their backs and their tails. We would then watch the brightly colored birds flicker from wooden peg to wooden peg within their wire cages, and search out the hamsters tucked away in their little plastic igloos, sleeping.

I watched Sophie approach Victor's animal. It was a rescue dog from Albany.

"Can I hug your dog?" Sophie asked. Lisa and I had taught her well: *Always ask the owner first. It's not your dog and you don't know how it will act.* Sophie understood. She never wanted to disappoint us.

"You sure can," said Victor. He was holding the dog firmly around the collar. It looked like a shepherd mix. Sophie was eye level with the dog. I saw her smile. I saw her lean in and hug the dog gently, putting her shoulder under the dog's muzzle. When she pulled back, the dog was soundless, as if studying her. And then, just like that, its mouth was attached to her face. Victor yanked back on the dog and Sophie stumbled backward. Our entire group was strangely silent, like a picture of all of us considering something important. Sophie's cheek fell open like a trap door. I could see her teeth behind, gleaming and white. Blood dropped from an opening in her neck and splashed across her chest and legs. She collapsed backward into the beautiful grass. That's when Lisa screamed. She was standing to my left and she screamed "Oh my god!" Her voice was terrible and wet and overwhelming and the only sound in the world. I took off my shirt. I stumbled forward and grabbed Sophie off the ground and pushed my shirt against her face. I then picked her up and held her. I pulled her small body against mine and turned back helpless toward the others.

*   *   *

Five millimeters. That's half a centimeter. It's the thickness of five credit cards stacked one on top of each other. It was also the distance between the dog bite in Sophie's neck and her carotid artery. Five millimeters more to the right and she would have bled out in my arms in less than three minutes. Also, the fact that her cheek had not fully torn off was something of a miracle.

"Your daughter is very lucky," the doctor said to Lisa and me. He had kind eyes and spoke to us in a warm, reassuring tone. The doctor had been in surgery with Sophie for over four hours, stitching Sophie's right cheek back in place and sewing closed the gash under her chin and in her neck. He explained the procedure slowly and clearly.

"How is she doing? Is she still asleep?" Lisa asked. Her throat was raw, her voice husky.

"Is she in her room yet?" I needed to know.

"She is still in recovery," The doctor said. "Yes, she is asleep and comfortable."

Before he went into surgery with our daughter, after the EMTs had us fill out forms and Victor stood next to me outside the waiting room sobbing and apologizing, I had asked the doctor how bad the bite was, how bad Sophie was hurt. What I really wanted to know was if she would ever be able to recover from this—if we, as a family, would ever be able to recover.

The doctor was a plastic surgeon and had performed hundreds of reconstructive surgeries in the past. "On a scale of one to ten, ten being the worst, I'd say she is a six," he said.

Six bothered me. Six was worse than five, and five seemed like it was on the very edge of what was manageable. Six, I believed, would not be manageable.

*   *   *

They let us sleep at the hospital that night. Gracie stayed at home with her grandparents, Lisa's folks having made the three-hour trip over from New Hampshire earlier that evening.

Lisa and I shared the small bed next to Sophie's and took turns waking up and crying. There was nothing else to be done, and I think we both knew that we were so deeply submerged in our own pain that comfort from each other could not resolve a thing. It was one of the most grueling nights of my life.

When I'd wake up, I'd forget for a minute where I was, but then I'd look over at Sophie quiet and buried under so many wires and tubes and I'd just slump back down on the little bed and squeeze my eyes with my fingers, grimace, and let out a couple of helpless sobs. Once, I woke up and saw Lisa standing next to Sophie, looking down at her in the half darkness. Though she was quiet, I knew Lisa was crying because her shoulders were rocking in this grievous, violent way, as if she was trying to control her entire body from exploding.

I didn't dream much that night, except once, right before dawn. In the dream, I was holding Sophie's bike by the seat, running alongside and trying to encourage her to peddle. We were in Miami. The sun was glorious and the walkway we raced down glowed bone-white.

"Come on, Sophie. You got it? You got it?! I'm going to let go!"

My heart was pounding out of my chest and I thought we both might lift off and fly.

Sophie was humming, and would not respond.

"You got this?" I asked again, but less sure.

I kept running but the bike became unruly; I could hear the gears catching and could sense the wheels spinning in these faintly bent orbits. Then the gears were the only thing I could hear, their grinding and crunching endless. So I ran harder, now almost pushing the bike. I focused on the white path. I was terrified to look anywhere else. If I looked at the bike—at Sophie—I didn't know what I would see, so I kept running.

*   *   *

Jim had been a close friend for about ten years by the time my family and I moved up to the Berkshires. We originally met at a school dedicated to helping teenagers rebuild their lives. I taught there because it was the first real job I was offered after earning my Master's degree; Jim taught there because it was close to his house and he'd already obliterated any other real teaching option.

Twenty years my senior, Jim exuded the type of acumen and fortitude I hoped to possess someday. Kurt Vonnegut's doppelganger, Jim could recite whole chunks of *Paradise Lost* by heart and even sections of *Canterbury Tales* in Middle English. He lived alone in the same farmhouse he grew up in and was always generous, kind, and quick to laugh. He also liked to get rip-stomping drunk, snort cocaine, and blow shit up.

Jim was my kind of guy.

Jim had once been a wunderkind of academia, teaching English Lit at Emerson College at the age of twenty-one. But after years of heavy drinking, and a particularly gruesome second divorce, Jim found it harder and harder to maintain steady employment until the choice teaching gigs at elite universities simply dried up. By the time we met, Jim had been teaching a couple of night classes at a community college in Holyoke to sustain himself.

But none of that mattered when we got together at his house. Sometimes Lisa would join us and we'd bring along the girls. Jim loved Sophie and Grace, and doted like a fussy uncle. We'd all sit outside near one of his herb gardens and sip gin and tonics, grilled chicken turning the air smoky and sweet. A stony river perfect for trout fishing rushed nearby and if it was warm enough we'd take the girls down for a swim, watch them grimace when they stuck a bare foot into the frigid water.

On nights that I dropped by alone it was a different story: We'd sit in his kitchen downing tumblers of Armagnac while debating whose proclivity for bad behavior was more forgivable, Robert Frost or Robert Lowell. We'd divide up the pills he scored from his friend in Northampton: *twenty Xanax for you, fifteen Vicodin for me*. Sometimes he'd save a gram or two of coke from his friend in New Bedford—an esteemed English professor at a big university—and we'd do it all and then go outside to shoot off his guns. Once, Jim plugged his old projection wide-screen television into an extension cord and we wheeled the whole thing out onto his lawn. *The Verdict* with Paul Newman was playing loudly on a VHS tape. Jim thankfully did not have any neighbors.

"Give it to him, Paul!" Jim shouted and then unloaded his shotgun into the screen. I jumped back in exalted terror, absolutely thrilled.

When we arrived in the Berkshires for the new jobs, we planned to meet at Jim's house for dinner, a kind of "welcome back" thing, so I phoned the night before to say hi and see if he had a few Percocet. It felt so natural.

"Yeah, yeah. No problem," he said.

I thought he might inquire why I wanted back on Percs, but the question never came.

"Great. Same price?"

"Plan on five bucks a pill. You know, *the usual*." Jim ended his sentence in a long, exaggerated lisp; it was something he did when in a good mood.

"Cool. Oh, anything I should bring to dinner? You all set?"

"I got it covered. Just don't forget to bring your three beautiful ladies," he said.

*   *   *

On the third day, the police contacted us to let us now that they finally had possession of the dog and that it was scheduled to be euthanized. Jim's offer of the handgun was thankfully no longer an option. Strangely, Victor's wife had brought the dog to her mother's house the day after the attack and I couldn't help but think that it was like she was harboring a fugitive, like hiding a criminal at a safe house. Lisa and I grew incensed when we had heard what the wife did and asked the school for help locating the dog. The school promised they would do everything they could.

On the fourth day, Sophie was allowed to leave the hospital. It was a quiet affair. When we arrived home, she put her many new stuffed animals on her bed. Sophie lined them up neatly in a row against the wall. She then cried and talked about how everything was different, and that her animals knew this and were all very sad. We listened and acknowledged how hard everything had been, but emphasized that change was only temporary and that Sophie had a family that loved her very much and would never abandon her. Then we hugged her, but carefully and tenderly. Afterward, Lisa went in the bathroom and cried, not wanting to show Sophie how terrified and helpless she actually felt.

During the first couple of days, we all tried to act normal. But Sophie's face was blighted in surgical tape, and under the tape, stitches ran a deep, puffy "C" around her cheek. We'd smile and talk and ask what she wanted for dinner or if she wanted to watch one of her favorite shows, but we all felt this great pall that we could neither shake nor name.

Victor called me and asked if he and his wife could come over and see Sophie, bring a present and apologize for what happened. I didn't want to see either of them, but Lisa and I figured it might be important to Sophie, so we relented.

They brought Sophie a life-sized stuffed pony that was gold and floppy and placed it in front of her in the living room; Sophie reached out and drew her fingers down the soft mane indifferently. Victor and his wife then stumbled through an awkward speech about how sorry they were and that it wasn't her fault that the dog bit her, etc. At this point, Victor's wife started to tear up.

"You know Sophie, I understand how precious life is, how it can change in an instant."

I couldn't tell where she was going.

Then the wife grimaced and put her hand to her mouth: "Because I had cancer once. And when you get cancer everything stops, everything changes."

Victor rubbed his wife's shoulder softly. "She did," he said.

I wanted to stand up and scream in their faces but Lisa and I sat there, stunned into silence.

Afterward, we shook hands at the door and they both left. Outside of classroom responsibility, we never interacted with them again.

*   *   *

By the end of the week, something spooky started to happen with Sophie.

During meals, the four of us trying to get down whatever it was on our plates, Sophie would stop what she was doing and go into a trance, just kind of stare off into space. Then she'd turn to us and say "What's your name?"

The first time this happened we all looked over at Sophie, a bit confused and wondering if she was playing a game. And this questioning would continue at mealtime, on and off, for about ten days.

"Name? What do you mean, Sophie?" Lisa asked, wiping her mouth with a napkin.

I put my fork down and looked at Sophie.

"What's your name?" she repeated.

"What do you mean, sweetie?" I asked.

"What's your name?"

Then she turned back to her plate and picked up her fork and pushed the peas around a little bit and stabbed a chunk of chicken, placing it in her mouth and chewing like nothing had happened.

After a few episodes like this, Lisa and I spoke about our options.

"The doctor said weird stuff like this might happen, but I don't know, Chris."

"Do you think we should call someone?" I asked.

"I don't know. I just…I don't know." Lisa's eyes welled and I understood; we were all freefalling, and there was no one, nothing, to catch us.

*   *   *

The next morning, still in my boxers, I looked at the few remaining pills I had hidden in my sock drawer and felt disgusted; I couldn't believe I had let go of myself so completely again. The only thing Sophie needed right now was a father and to feel safe and I chose instead to run directly into the flames. I felt like I was going to throw up.

Lisa came in the room and I looked over at her, closed the drawer abruptly.

"What's wrong?" she asked.

"Nothing. I'm just…I'm just overwhelmed."

"You look freaked out."

"It's because *I am* a freak." I smiled weakly, stepped away from the drawer and moved closer to her.

Lisa stared at me one beat too long.

"When we went over to Jim's last week, before all this bullshit happened, did he give you pills?"

"What? Of course not. No. Why would you ask that?"

"Because if that is something you've chosen to do I don't think I could handle it, Chris. I don't think I could have you around here with us." Her voice had risen dramatically.

"Lisa, you just need to relax and calm down, okay?"

"I swear to God, Chris, I won't deal with all that crap again. I won't!"

"You know what? Back off! What's wrong with you?"

"Yeah, I'll back off, you fucking asshole!"

Lisa turned and stormed out. I blinked and stood momentarily, considering my options. Stupidly, I decided to follow her.

By the time I rounded the long hallway and made my way into the dining room, I could hear Sophie and Grace arguing in the kitchen.

"No," said Sophie. "Give it."

"That's mine, Sophie. You already had one," Grace said.

"Girls, stop it," Lisa said.

I stopped next to the dining room table and listened, unable to see what was happening.

"No," Sophie yelled.

"I said it's mine," Grace countered.

"Girls, girls…OH MY GOD!"

I bolted into the kitchen, wild and scared to death. It was Lisa. She had just screamed *Oh My God* exactly the same way she did right after Sophie was attacked.

"WHAT?! WHAT IS IT?!" I bellowed, looking wildly about the room.

All three looked up at me, startled.

"Chris, Jesus, what's wrong?" Lisa was frightened.

"Why would you do that?" I demanded. Sophie flinched.

"Do what?"

"I thought Grace was hurting Sophie! I thought...I thought she was ripping out her stitches! What the hell is going on?! Why are you screaming 'Oh my God'?!"

Lisa looked me in the eyes.

"Chris," she said. "I didn't scream anything. No one said anything at all."

*   *   *

PTSD is a bitch. As my first and only experience with it, what I find incredible is how *real* Lisa's voice sounded—I would have bet my left arm that her voice came from the kitchen and that she was truly screaming. I could hear it as something separate from me, not in my head.

When I spoke to my friend Ken on the phone about it that night—he worked with an agency that helped foreign victims of torture adjust to life in the US—he said he heard stories like mine all the time. Even worse.

"Sometimes those recovering from trauma will even act out the traumatic experience again, exactly how they remembered it. They'll then sort of wake up, not aware they went into a trance at all."

Partly I didn't want to accept that this had happened to me, that I had succumbed to a kind of psychological blood-letting; or even more troubling: that I was damaged worse than I thought.

"But it was so real," I said, still trying to bargain my way out.

Ken understood. "That's because it *was* real," he said.

*   *   *

When I got up the next morning, Lisa had taken the girls and gone to a check-up for Sophie; I had completely forgotten about the appointment and overslept. I found a note from Lisa in the kitchen:

Chris,
We need to talk tonight. I love you!
Lisa xoxo

After reading the note several times, I threw it away. Not because I didn't agree we needed to talk, but because I was worried that if Gracie found the note and read it, she'd understand that I let everyone down somehow.

I poured a bowl of Lucky Charms and decided to call Jim on his cell. He said he was on his way back from Albany and could stop by. I told him to meet me at the bagel shop in town. I figured I might be meeting up with him to buy another handful of pills. I also thought I might be meeting to say I could no longer see him anymore if it involved drugs. Both scenarios scared me.

Jim sat idling in the parking lot his silver GMC pickup. I parked across from him, nodded through the windshield, and got out.

When I sat in the front cab with him, I could smell his woodstove and spilled motor oil. We chatted a bit about Sophie, the school, etc., and then the conversation turned.

"So, what's happening?"

"Nothing. Just trying to cope, you know," I said.

"Yeah, I know."

"Lisa totally freaked out on me yesterday."

"Really? Why?"

"She's so... I don't know." I breathed sharply out of my nose. "I've got to lay low on the pills. Lay off, I guess."

"Well, that's a good thing. Sure."

"No, you're right, it is. But I just can't stand everything right now, you know? It's all so fucking bleak and final. Everything. I mean, for fuck's sake, Jim, we just moved here! I haven't even started teaching yet. I wanted to make such a good impression. I don't know how to restart this thing. And Sophie, well..."

Jim was nodding and looking down at the steering wheel, just trying to stay out of my way.

"What would you do?" I asked.

"About what?"

I smiled. "I don't know." I didn't know any other way out in that moment. "Never mind. I just gotta get my head on right. You know me."

"Chris…"

"Jim, it was good seeing you, my man. Really." I put my hand on his shoulder and squeezed. I thought I was about to cry. "But Lisa should be home soon. I'll call you tonight. Thanks for stopping. Sorry I'm being so dramatic or whatever. Talk to you soon."

But I didn't call him that night. Or again for a long while after. I got out of his truck for the last time that day. And though we still saw each other sporadically after that, it wasn't quite the same. It couldn't be.

Five years later, standing with a small group of family and friends, we would spread his ashes freely atop one of the great fields running his property. Jim died while sitting at his kitchen table opening mail; a heart attack. Many spoke that day about the kind, funny, and generous man they loved and remembered, but I chose to not to speak, chose rather to listen. On the way home, I held Lisa's hand while I drove and remembered the Jim that I had loved: the one standing loose and easy on his lawn, happy, sober, trying to help my daughters pick tarragon for the first time from his garden, overly protective as they awkwardly stretched and grabbed the leaves, his hands hovering behind their backs while he said: "Careful, girls. Whoops, that's right, you got it. Careful, honey."

＊　　＊　　＊

It was my turn to read Sophie a story that night and put her to bed. I first got her teeth brushed, a game where I played the dentist Dr. Pop and she my willing patient. I slowly brushed her teeth next to the sink and asked how she had been since our last visit. She said she'd been well but that her cheek hurt lately. "Oh, I'm sorry to hear that. Will everything be okay?" I asked in my Dr. Pop voice.

"I think so," Sophie said through the foam.

I took extra precautions and brushed gently on that side of her mouth, smiling while looking her in the eyes.

I suddenly flashed to when Sophie was admitted to the hospital, her little body piled on top of the gurney and about to be wheeled into surgery. Lisa and I knew it would be the last time we'd see her before they took her away. We stood gripping the edge of the gurney, helpless. I looked down at her and told her I was sorry, that I was so sorry for what had happened.

Sophie looked up at me and swallowed, and when she swallowed, a little stream of blood flowed out of the opening in her neck and onto the crinkly white paper underneath her and Sophie continued looking up at me and then lifted her hand to my face and said "It's okay, Papa." At the very moment I couldn't believe her strength and was overwhelmed by her bravery in the face of my human panic and basic smallness.

I blinked the image away, adjusted myself, and then asked "So, young lady, are we ready to rinse?"

In her room, Sophie had one pile of books that her mom read from, and a smattering of others that I could pick from without repercussions. I flipped through a couple but none was particularly jumping out.

"Mind if I tell you a story tonight, Soph, instead of reading one?"

"That'd be nice, Papa."

I turned all the lights off except her star nightlight and we lay down across her bed. The dark soothed me and I felt my breath come in steady, even waves. Sophie's breathing slowed down, thickened.

"Have I told you the one about the Night Faerie?"

"Uh-ah."

Sophie loved fairies. She had copious books about them, detailing the different types that existed throughout the world, what they ate, where they lived, which flowers or trees they were associated with, if they were good or, on the rare occasion, bad.

When Sophie and I took walks through the woods, we'd sometimes exclusively look for fairy houses. We would eventually end up at some opening at the base of a tree and investigate if it was a suitable habitat for a fairy or even a whole family of them. If the space looked particularly promising, we'd place some sticks and leaves at the opening, a soft piece of moss or just-picked trillium, maybe an overturned acorn cap as makeshift water basin. Sometimes, I would return alone to the spot and leave Sophie a handwritten note from the fairies on the back of a little scrap of birch bark, thanking her, saying that they loved her and were always watching over her.

The next day, I'd find a reason to tromp with her back to the tree, and watch her fill with joy as she made her discovery. In those moments, I felt like one of the dads I'd read about in parenting books and saw in Disney-fied movies: the kind that didn't know how to disappoint and only knew how to make good decisions.

"Where's the Night Faerie?" Sophie asked, curling the pillow under her head.

"Well, the Night Faerie lived alone on top of Mt. Washington. He didn't understand why the other fairies got all the attention just because they lived amongst the daylight and the blackberry bushes. Night Faerie had an important job too: he needed to make sure all the stars spun correctly over our heads, and that the moon lit our paths between the shadows so we wouldn't stumble or get lost."

"That's an important job," Sophie reasoned.

"It is! And so Night Faerie kept doing what he was doing, working…"

"Wait. Did he live alone?"

"Well, yeah."

"Why?"

"He just… he was different. And he knew he was different. But he knew he had love to give, that, that, his love was thorny and maybe a little rusty, but that it was there nonetheless."

Sophie thought a good while about this.

"Pop," she finally asked.

"Yeah?"

"Why was his love 'thorny'?"

I smiled up into the darkness and then turned toward my daughter.

"Because sometimes it was hidden from him. But he wants to practice at not hiding. He wants to practice...better."

"That's good," said Sophie.

I reached and placed my open palm against Sophie's face, but softly, and with her little hand she held my wrist, then let go. And as I lie there, I could imagine a pack of Night Faeries digging out from underneath their rocks, their small piles of sticks and wood, brushing at their shorn garments and capes, if that's what they wore, and turning their attention to the sky, their job at keeping it aloft, keeping it from pummeling our bodies and our heads. The image kind of scared me and I was surprised how frightened I was.

I could not come that close to losing Sophie again because my love for her was greater than the sum of me. And I also understood those things in my life that were not love must begin their terrible unhooking: "Goodbye," they would say. "Goodbye." I could not heed their cries.

I breathed deep. I would not bargain or plead; Lisa was waiting in the living room and would need to know the truth. I shifted uneasily as all around me the house took up with the wind and went about its business of settling and leaning, pressing its wooden frame, like a small ache, into the dark.

With You

Google says prolapsed hemorrhoid, so I wait my turn, standing, in the ER. I'm led to a smaller room and am greeted by a physician assistant and her student. They lay me on my side, hospital gown like sloughed skin. Brief exam, knees to chest. Awkward embarrassment. Usual jokes. Ha, ha, ha. Thrombosis has swollen to the size of an almond. PA says it must be lanced, and the clot removed.

Small fears lattice my ribs, tighten the chords in my neck. I roll onto my stomach. This is going to hurt, she says. Dripping needle injected straight into the most sacred area on my backside. I gasp, eyes water. The student holds my buttocks apart so the PA can do her job. She cuts, squeezes out the clot. There we go, she says. Blood down my thighs, pools at my hipbones. All done. Victory. Everybody jokes again. You like beer? student says. Well, you'll probably want one tonight. Or two! I wince. Gauze pushed up and between my legs. You'll be fine, PA says. Rest a few minutes.

Alone, facedown, I wonder if I should call someone. I then feel warmth pumping slowly across my ass. I sit up: the sheet's growing sticky red. The call bell doesn't work so I swing my legs out and over, limp to the door and chirp at a gaggle of uniforms crowding the Nurses' Station. Blood spatters my feet like I'm a red house painter, streaks down my legs in an attempt to one-up gravity. I get back on my cot, notice a single pearl of red on my knee-cap—ladybug defrocked of her spots. I smile at the notion.

They come back in. No problem, no problem. We're here. More gauze, "quick clot" medicinal patch applied. Grimacing on my stomach, blood continues its lazy bubbling. Different hands apply pressure. Then more pressure. Tighter. Bleeding continues. We're going to have to cauterize, she says. Another doctor enters the room. Silver nitrate is pushed into the wound and I cry out, my head lighter than wings made of fog. My right hand is wet and I leave three red fingerprints on my pillow. I smell iron. Now they are talking like I'm not there: You see, it won't stop oozing. Yes, yes. That's because it's bleeding internally, see? Get more gauze. Did you get more gauze?

Panic collapses into something close to terror. Not like this, I think. Not here. I close my eyes. Another doctor enters the room. The air is warmer, thicker. I need to pass out, but instead think about my wife and daughters. Focus hard on their faces, I tell myself. Focus. See them. Summer backyard last June when we lolled about the grass, laughed because the sun clattered atop our heads in bright joy. Our shoulders touched. The air was sweet with grill smoke. And the tomatoes we planted made our hands smell wild, nearly green.

That is when they lift my body higher, off the damp sheet and onto a table. Light fills in the darker spaces, and I will understand what it means to be saved.

Fleeting

"Essays, like poems and stories and novels, marry heaven and hell."

—Donald Hall

I was in New Hampshire when I learned Donald Hall had died. Fitting, as that's where he'd spent the last forty years of his life, and where I was born. I was a passenger in the family car, Grace and Sophie asleep in the back. Lisa drove silently; we were in a fight and not talking. Our silence crowded the small air between us. I was absently scrolling Facebook on my phone when WHAM: a giant of American letters and former US Poet Laureate, Donald Hall, was gone. Reading the post a second time my breath hitched. And then I closed my eyes.

I placed the phone face down on my lap. My last letter to Don had remained unanswered; now I knew why. Don and I have been writing each other, on and off, for almost twenty-five years. Ironically, we had never met, but our camaraderie seemed to grow with every letter.

He died on Saturday, June 23, 2018. And now, less than twenty-four hours later, I pressed my head against the passenger window of our Subaru, not sure what to say, or to whom. As if on cue, a light rain began skidding across the glass. You've got to be kidding me, I thought.

My family was returning home to the Adirondacks after a much-needed vacation. It had been a glorious week of dry days and azure skies on the beaches of Maine. But a rather nasty fight between me and Lisa that morning remained unresolved. It was a completely different vibe in the car than from a week ago, which was a ride filled with chatter and laughter and light.

Lisa flicked the wipers to accommodate the building rain. I didn't want to tell her, didn't really know *how* to tell her. Besides, I was still mad, still hurt from our disagreement. I shifted uncomfortably in my seat as thoughts bounced between the shock of learning about Don's death and my very first memories of him. My throat grew hot and I acquiesced.

"Hey Lisa," I said. "You won't believe the news."

*   *   *

In 1994, Lisa and I backpacked through Central America. For several days, we stayed at a small hostel called *Tres Hermanas* ("three sisters") in Nebaj, Guatemala; Nebaj was a former stronghold for the rebels during Guatemala's civil war of the mid-twentieth century. The Mayan people of Nebaj experienced great suffering at the hands of the government during this time.

On our last night in *Tres Hermanas*, I heard a woman in our room say that she was afraid because the house was on fire. I heard this clearly and in English. Lisa and I were the only guests in the hostel at the time. I nudged Lisa next to me, hoping she was talking in her sleep.

"Lisa, why are you saying the house is on fire?" I asked.

"Go back to sleep," Lisa said. "You're dreaming."

The next morning, during a breakfast of eggs and toast and instant coffee in the garden, I felt relieved in the daylight, and asked Lisa why she seemed unfazed after I told her I heard someone talking in our room. And in perfect English.

"Because I heard the voice too," she said.

"You did?"

"Yeah, only I heard it in Spanish. I thought if we kept talking it would only encourage the ghost."

After Lisa's admission, I was a little freaked out and decided an hour of quiet reading would ground me. At the time, I carried only three books in my rucksack: a copy of the literary journal the *Gettysburg Review*; Alan Lightman's *Einstein's Dreams*; and Donald Hall's memoir *Life Work*. I sought refuge in Don's book that day, sitting by a koi pond in the *Tres Hermanas* garden. The mountain air was thin and the sun sharp. Reading a few pages leveled me out, and the experience from the night before grew more ephemeral and distant with each turned page.

As far as memoirs go, *Life Work* is short, barely over one hundred pages. I picked up a paperback copy for the trip, not having read any of Don's prose at that point. During my six months on the road, I snatched paragraphs here and there when I could. I ended up reading the book twice, as did Lisa. It became our go-to during arduous bus rides to remote cloud forests or after lunch on non-travel days, whiling away the hours in the Central American heat.

Life Work is a deeply felt meditation on the value of authentic labor. For Don, that meant choosing to be a writer, and not wavering from that path. He meticulously detailed his life and his writing process while living in the New Hampshire home his grandfather bought in the nineteenth century. I swooned, so wanting the life he described. And not only was it a love letter to the written word, it was an actual love letter to his second wife, Jane Kenyon. An acclaimed poet herself, her collection *Constance* would prove critical in my own development as a writer. Their shared days of quiet writing and revision, coupled with their habitual midday amorous entwinings, followed by yet more diligent writing and revision until dusk, seemed the perfect recipe to me on how to live.

But the most surprising thing about the book is the abrupt turn it takes halfway through; Don learns he has colon cancer, which then spreads to his liver, and the deep weight of mortality takes hold of his prose, and he starts second guessing if he's used his timely wisely enough to write all the things he knows he needs to write, done all the things he needs to do. And this from someone already so prolific and celebrated. The cruel twist in the book is that he states he won't live another ten years, but it's Jane that dies young, contracting leukemia and dying just a few years after the publication of *Life Work*. She was forty-seven. Don went on to live almost thirty more years after his own prognosis and died at the age eighty-nine.

I had originally been introduced to Don's work when I was an undergraduate—specifically his book of poems *Kicking the Leaves*. I grew to love the fact that there was a famous poet actually living in my tiny home state. *Well, I better introduce myself to him*, I thought: *Poet to poet*, and began corresponding with Don the week after I graduated.

At first, I gushed like any old fan, but after a couple of letters I shared that I had grown up in Exeter. Don attended Philips Exeter Academy for two years, a time he later described to me as "the most wretched in (his) life." He loved that I told him I was a townie and had only dated the academy girls to spite the academy boys.

I later sent a batch of poems and proclaimed I sought no praise (though I surely did) and he was gracious in his remarks, bestowing words of encouragement and hope. He knows a poet just starting out in his twenties usually looks for approval and guidance from the old guard, even though they'll be too cool to admit it. "You've got something here, and I appreciate the energy in these poems," he said.

I stood in the kitchen of my apartment in Portsmouth, reading and rereading those words, and cared little to hide my joy.

*   *   *

We crossed into Vermont via Lebanon, New Hampshire, and I grew restless. Lisa was tired and needed a break from driving. I suggested an upcoming rest stop.

"Not yet," she said without looking at me. "I'm fine."

Lisa's words had the weight of accusation, but I didn't engage. Instead, I glanced over my shoulder at the girls. Both were now awake and beholders of similar expressions—earbuds and indifference. I turned back around and briefly considered Lisa's silhouette, remembered a happier time when we were in Guanajuato for six months back in 2012.

Towards the end of that stay, Don published an essay in the *American Scholar* about a trip to Europe he took in the fifties with his first wife, Kirby. The piece was both telling and sad, but rich with detail. Kirby too died of cancer, just like Jane, but Don was grateful her illness brought him and Kirby back together after many years of estrangement. I read the essay all at once one morning in bed, the house to myself as the girls were all off to Spanish class. The ending made me cry, particularly because of this line in the last paragraph: *But there are no happy endings, because if things are happy, they have not ended.* A year later, I'd ask Don to borrow that line as an epigraph for a poem I was working on about the complexities of my own marriage. But that day, I sent Don an email to let him know how moving the essay was, and how it affected me so deeply way down here in Mexico.

Don's reply came quick and filled with verve. He was grateful for my email, and discussed his own time spent in Mexico in the nearby city of San Miguel de Allende. In fact, it turned out we were both in San Miguel the same year (2007) for two different writing festivals: one where I taught a poetry workshop in the spring and the other in the fall where he went to simply be "fawned over and celebrated." Not a bad deal, I told him.

I shared new poems, and of one in particular he said "...fills every rift with ore." With his own tip of the hat to Keats, I was overcome by such high praise. But he didn't always love what I wrote, once calling an image of mine "metaphor-chowder." Fair enough, I thought, and quickly scrubbed the lines clean.

We exchanged travel stories: he tales of India with Jane, and me about my naïve adventurism on another occasion in Mexico during the Zapatista uprising when I was almost shot point blank in the face by a soldier. Don loved that one. He told me new essays were coming out in the *New Yorker* and *Playboy* and I joked that I could finally say I was reading *Playboy* for the articles and actually mean it.

In another letter, Don expressed that poetry had left him, and that he was no longer writing poems. But he didn't see it as a loss. He was still pumping out essays; he had said everything he needed to say in poetry. But still, I was saddened to learn the news. At eighty-two, this struck me as perhaps his first step off the proverbial mortal coil, but I kept that observation to myself.

A few years later, solidly back home and teaching English again, I wrote Don about two new books I had forthcoming, both about Mexico. One was a collection of poems, the other poems and essays about Guanajuato. I beat around the bush and finally asked sheepishly if he'd offer a blurb. I was surprised to learn it was his policy never to write them.

"Back in 1960—I do believe!—I decided never to write another blurb. I had written a few, which were terrible, and so were most people's. The last one I wrote was for X.J. Kennedy with whom I workshopped in Ann Arbor. Since then, I've told my poet friends about my decision—at least ten thousand times—and I can't change my mind at this point."

I thanked him anyway, and as I was serving as the nonfiction editor for a literary magazine out of Brooklyn, I had another idea about how we might be able to collaborate: I asked if he had any essays he might want to offer us for publication. We paid a modest fee, but I hoped Don would appreciate the earnestness with which I made my pitch; many notable writers spoke highly of our magazine and I shared their words.

He said yes, but that he had only two essays remaining from his forthcoming collection that had not been placed in magazines. Yet neither of those two would do, he said. He proposed a compromise.

"I am writing a tiny essay which might do well for you, and would not do for the *New Yorker* et cetera. My editor asked me to write a piece, something short to be printed between the first essay and the next. It's about going from poetry to prose, and the pleasures of prose, and hints about writing memoir. I think it might do for (your magazine), with a note saying how it was conceived, and that it will be part of the collection. I'm still working on it, and I might take another month. (I have only written twenty drafts.) Then let us see."

A month later, he had his assistant email me the finished piece, called "From Poems to Paragraphs," which was really a collection of flash-essays operating as anecdotes and insights detailing his revision process; all of his essays went through a minimum of thirty drafts, some eighty. As promised, he also discussed his change to writing solely prose. "Originally I wrote 'poetry suddenly left me' which after twelve drafts became 'poetry abandoned me'—with another sentence to avoid self-pity." His wit and humor were as sharp and observant as ever, and the piece just sang. I was eminently grateful, but to Don, eh, no big deal. "Glad you liked the piece," was all he said. Incidentally, when the book came out, the name of the essay was changed to the title of the collection itself: *Essays After Eighty.* I couldn't have been more proud.

*   *   *

Lisa bisected Vermont's Green Mountains slowly and with care. At one point, we stopped behind a Honda Accord marooned in the middle of the road. The rain had finally let up and everything glistened. We inched around slowly, the driver excitedly pointing while mouthing the word "Moose" behind the glass at me.

We didn't see anything, but later read in the paper that an albino moose was galloping through the area at the time. Something that large and that white must have looked absolutely terrifying. I thought of Ahab and smiled.

We finally made our way into Bread Loaf, a rather strange collection of yolk-colored houses lining either side of the road just outside of Middlebury. You already know enough about the writing conference—even *The Simpsons* has parodied it. Don was accepted to Bread Loaf when he was a teenager. He once wrote to me: "I went to Breadloaf (sic) in 1945 when I was 16. Can you imagine what it feels like to write that sentence?"

So how perfect was it that I dropped my cell phone between the seats and couldn't reach it as we drove by, me cursing softly, finally unbuckling my seatbelt and grabbing wildly to no avail.

"Jesus, let me pull over," Lisa said.

I opened the door and got out, dropped to my knees on the damp asphalt. I finally grabbed my iPhone and pulled it free, slicing the top of my hand as I did.

Wincing, I stood up catching my breath, and took all of Bread Loaf in in that moment: the wide and perfect green lawns, a couple walking by arm in arm, those strangely yellowed houses. And then I imagined Don as fresh-faced teenager in search of a voice, standing alone on one of the wraparound porches beside me.

I suddenly wanted to cry. I felt his loss like the Vermont air pressing my skin and filling my lungs. I knew in that moment that I didn't tell him everything that I wanted to, or that I should have. Though we spoke about solitude at length, I didn't ask him enough questions about loneliness, or if he feared death. I didn't say simple things like, *Hey man, how the hell are you?* and instead fretted if my letters were "poetic enough." I felt I had once again found a way to squander something important and there wasn't a damn thing anyone could do about it, least of all me. He once asked that I call him so we could arrange a time to get together, saying that he "so wanted to meet me," but I was busy, busy, busy, traveling from one country to the next, thinking *Yeah, yeah, I will. Later.* I had now run out of laters.

"Chris, are you okay?" Lisa asked, leaning over the passenger seat and speaking up to me.

I ran my hand through my hair. Would this be my stupid fate? Would I just keep fucking things up, over and over, until I had nothing left? I looked back at my wife, my love, and thought how lucky I was to have this woman in my life all these years.

"Um, yeah, I'm fine," I said. "Do you . . . do you need me to drive now?" Lisa smiled. But I didn't wait for her answer. I simply walked around the car and gently opened her door.

Corrections

"Who understands me when I say this is beautiful?"

—Jimmy Santiago Baca

I'd taught creative writing at all kinds of places, but during my new hire orientation at the federal prison, I was told that I needed to learn how to *be* a hostage if in fact I became one; I looked at the lieutenant addressing me and nodded thoughtfully, as if this was just regular new job housekeeping stuff I'd heard a zillion times.

I sat at a small desk for four hours as different personnel rotated in and out to let me know what I'd gotten myself into. It was clear I was there to listen, and the psychologist, the educational coordinator, the warden, and various COs all had their own take on prison life. Some were funny, many expressed hope. A few sounded like they didn't particularly like their jobs and I immediately began siding with the prisoners. At the end of the day, I was shown glossy photos of confiscated weapons, including shanks and zip guns.

"Tell them nothing about your personal life," the lieutenant said at one point. "Not where you live. Or if you're married. Or even if you have kids or not. Nothing."

After a tour of the classrooms, the education coordinator asked if I had any questions. He had a close-cropped beard and kind eyes.

"Yeah," I said. "Can I create a literary magazine with my students?"

*   *   *

On the first day of class I didn't know what to expect even though I thought I knew. After I signed in and handed over my keys and license, I was told to go through the metal detector but kept setting it off—first my belt, then my shoes. I was finally brought to the education center and handed a walkie talkie.

"That's the emergency button," the guard said pointing to a bright orange button on top. "Don't push it unless," he said.

"Unless what," I said.

"You'll know."

I entered my classroom and waited. I read and reread the roster; I wanted to make sure I got their names right. My seven students arrived ten minutes later. We took turns shaking hands and introducing ourselves. I told them my name was Mr. Locke, as I was instructed: *Never tell them your first name.* And in turn, I was to refer to them only by their last names. Their age range seemed between twenty and fifty-five, and the older guy was carrying a beautiful prayer rug over his shoulder when we shook hands.

I handed out the syllabus after everyone took their seats. The room had no windows and everything was beige. I said we'd break the class down into two-week units, with the first unit focusing on poetry. I asked if anyone had ever written a poem. No one said a thing. Mr. Cruz kind of shook his head. The air was thick and a fan hummed uselessly in the corner. I started sweating.

Mr. Cruz spoke up. "I write some free verse. I like blank verse too. But yeah, I really dig meter."

"Meter?" asked Mr. Delgado.

"Yeah, meter. Rhyme. Iambic pentameter. We talked about this," said Mr. Cruz.

"Why do they call poems 'verse'?" asked Mr. Foote. He had thin, short dreads, oval wire-rimmed glasses. His eyes were clear.

"Well, um, sure, poems are sometimes called 'verse.' But verse actually means 'turn,'" I said.

I thought for a second and then had an idea. I opened my textbook.

"I'd like to read you guys a poem to start things off," I said. "And after I read, let's see if we can find a part of the poem that illustrates a turn, or a kind of hinge, swinging us away from the current action and into something new."

I read the poem out loud. The name of the poem or who wrote it doesn't matter. I was so nervous I just hoped I could get through it without them all laughing at me.

Afterward, I asked that they read it again to themselves and think about my question and then mark the poem at the place, or places, a turn occurs. My students wrote and wrote. There was great seismographic scratching that I found exceptionally pleasing. Finally, one student raised his hand.

"Yes, Mr. Delgado," I said.

"I thought poems were supposed to rhyme," he said.

"No, not all poems," I said.

He considered my reply carefully. "Will we write poems like this?" he asked.

"I would like that," I said.

*   *   *

Over the following week we read out loud poems by Gary Soto, Carolyn Forché, and Brian Turner. We talked about the art of linguistic compression and the importance of energy—how one trims language down to the muscle. And because we read those three poets we also talked about baseball, Mexican immigration, and Caesar Chavez; El Salvador, civil war, and body dumps; the Iraq War, Islam, and when it was appropriate to say *Inshallah*.

Then it was time for them to read their villanelles; no one in class had ever written one, let alone read one out loud. And all they had as reference was Thomas' "Do not go gentle into that good night."

Mr. Delgado went first. He'd dropped out of school in the eighth grade. All his life he'd known poverty and gangs; white people crowding the sun off his beach back in Puerto Rico. His hands are overrun in tattoos of birds and ornate letters, eyes weeping across knuckles. He read his villanelle. It was tender, nearly sweet.

"This poem," he said. "All I could think about as I wrote it was love."

"What are you talking about?" joked Mr. Johnson, the youngest of my students. "You mean like...your girlfriend?" A couple of snickers. And all Mr. Delgado had to do was laugh back and he'd be off the hook. Vulnerability thwarted.

"No. I mean all kinds. Every kind. Just...love."

*   *   *

Class started late, as transfers were running behind. We would be without Mr. Johnson; he'd been caught up in a large fight and remanded to solitary confinement. I looked at his desk several times during class. It vibrated with his absence.

The students began reading their revised poems. They were originally scaffolded from a Bob Hicok poem, but we had dropped the scaffolding and they'd evolved into pieces more closely resembling their own voices. Mr. Cruz read his. Normally eager to speak and engage, Mr. Cruz read his poem merely louder than a breath. His poem recounted his years growing up in North Carolina. As he read, I could pick up the faintest hint of a southern accent, not something I had heard before.

"Damn, Charlie Brown (Mr. Cruz's nickname), that was all quiet and shit," said Mr. Leeds. "What happened to you?"

"I'm not proud," Mr. Cruz said.

"What?" said Mr. Foote.

"Where I'm from," Said Mr. Cruz. "I'm not proud."

Mr. Delgado got worked up. "Are you kidding me? I'm from Puerto Rico and I embrace that shit. You're a Mexican from the south and you feel...embarrassed?"

"Yeah. I guess so."

"You and me, Charlie Brown, we're having a talk, after class. You and me," said Mr. Delgado. He was pointing back and forth and his voice was enlarged. I knew he considered Mr. Cruz a brother.

After class, two other teachers and I were buzzed out of the education wing, walked alongside the fence with its tuft of razor wire, buzzed back inside, and then returned our walkie-talkies through a slot like the kind found at drive-thru pharmacies. We put our right hands under the blacklight so the officer could see the stamp we received that morning, and then we flipped the three red chits on a board back over to white, meaning we had left the prison. Then it was more waiting behind heavy doors, another buzzing, stepping inside a small room, our escort closing the door behind us, and waiting for the next door to be buzzed open. You moved like this in orchestrated segments: start, shuffle, stop, as if slowly making your way through a train's multiple cars.

Back outside in the parking lot, the sun was ruthless, piercing. We all complained. Unlocking the door to his Chevette, the business teacher told us he was just doing this gig for fun and that he used to make $200,000 on Wall Street.

Uh-huh, I thought. Sure you did.

*   *   *

Class was about to start, and Mr. Hamilton was steaming.

"You're steaming, Mr. Hamilton. What's up?" I asked.

"You know, these clowns don't know shit," he said. He stared right into me, his eyes gray and still as two dimes underwater. "I filled out my goddamn form requesting extra postage so I can mail out my letter and ten days later my counselor still hasn't approved it. It should take three fucking days. They're all lucky I don't have a gun with bullets," he said.

"Oh yeah? Maybe we're all lucky," I offered.

"I didn't say I'd kill him, just let him know the extent of my anger. Shoot off his goddamn big toe, throw him off balance so he has to limp around the rest of his life."

I looked down at the table and then back up, laughing. Mr. Hamilton laughed too, a big, booming laugh that said no matter how steep these walls, I can dream higher.

"No one has gone to hell just for shootin' someone in the ass," he said.

"Or toe," I reminded.

We laughed again.

*   *   *

After class, I waited with the students and other prisoners in a smallish day room—it resembled an elementary school cafeteria. I grabbed a seat at a table where three guys I didn't know were talking passionately, but just under the volume of normal conversation. They all nodded and said what's up.

"Hey," I said. I placed my books neatly in front of me, detached my walkie-talkie from my belt and laid it sideways on top of my pile.

"You teach that creative writing class, right?" one guy said. He had a round, open face and a perfectly symmetrical afro.

"Yeah."

"I heard that's hard."

I shrugged. "Eh, it's all perspective."

He tipped his head at me, returned to his conversation about his own college classes and which professors were good, which were assholes. I thankfully didn't hear my name.

I looked around while trying to look like I wasn't looking around. There were about forty guys in olive green jumpsuits milling about, waiting for the intercom and its charged voice granting permission for everyone to transfer back up the hill to their cells. White guys hung out with white guys, black guys with black, Hispanic with Hispanic. As the only white dude at the table, I wondered if my sitting there broke some kind of unspoken rule, or if I got a free pass because I was a teacher.

I began thinking about my past, stupid shit I did that could have landed me in a place like this: buying drugs, selling drugs. But mostly buying. *A lot.* There were times in college I had enough cocaine in my possession that, if busted, would have carried a mandatory minimum. The only difference between me and many of the men here is that I was lucky not to be in the wrong place at the wrong time. *Jesus Christ,* I thought. *Am I just prancing around like some clueless dickhead, giving off classic white savior vibes?*

After about twenty minutes, I realized I was the only non-prisoner in the room. I began feeling a little anxious for being alone this long, which was quickly followed by shame for feeling anxious. Everyone else was oblivious—talking, standing with their backs against the concrete walls, or sitting at tables. No one, rightfully, gave two shits I was there. Their voices blended into a kind of indiscernible hum, as if everything and nothing was at stake and great truths needed to be ferried through narrow passages.

I saw my escort—a guard name Susan—enter the room, keys bouncing at her hip. I stood up.

"Sit tight," she said. "You'll need to get comfortable for a while." I sat back down. She unlocked a door to an office and got on the phone. I watched her behind a large square of glass talk and nod her head affirmative. She came back out, closed and relocked the door. "We're going to be here a while," she said.

She moved past me in another jangle of keys and just like that was gone. I looked down at my roster sheet and pretended I was engaged in something very important. Fifteen more minutes went by. The guys maintained their conversation, used to these types of delays.

I stood up and stretched, imagined what would happen if I was required to stay all night, some urgent kind of lockdown out of my control. Where would I sleep, I thought.

"Hey," said the guy who asked me earlier if I taught creative writing.

"Yeah?"

"What do you suggest I use if I want a guide or whatever to help me with my writing?"

"You want this book," I said, and slid over my textbook.

"Does it have short stories?" he asked.

"We just read one in class today by a guy named Michael Cunningham, "White Angel." It's an incredible story," I said. "Beautiful, actually."

"Oh yeah?"

"Yeah," I said.

And he found the story in the table of contents, turned to the page, and started to read.

*   *   *

"When I Was Sixteen, I Knew It Was A Lie That…"

That was the essay prompt. I told them nothing else except this: "Be brave."

Mr. Leeds, who generally writes in an earnest pastiche of clichés, wrote that When I Was Sixteen I knew It Was A Lie that Santa Claus came down our chimneys because there weren't any chimneys in the 'hood. Some white man bringing us presents? Please. We'd rob HIM if given the chance. The only white men we saw were cops, and the kind of presents they brought were the ones we didn't want.

Mr. Cruz wrote that When I Was Sixteen I Knew It Was A Lie that everything would be all right. The night his mom was to leave the hospital he slept in her bed because the way her pillow smelled like the strawberry shampoo she loved so much lulled him to sleep. When the banging door woke him up all he could think was how mad he was that sleep was ruined until his neighbor met him at the door to tell him that his mother had died before she could be released.

And then it was Mr. Delgado's turn to read.

"It's, it's no big deal. Just my thoughts," he said.

"No," said Mr. Foote. "It's your truth."

Mr. Delgado smiled and then looked down at his paper. It did not shake or move.

"When I Was Sixteen I Knew It Was A Lie that I could be loved." And then bravely, just as I had asked, he continued.

*   *   *

On the final day of class Mr. Cruz lingered so we could talk. I'd already informed the men that we wouldn't be able to create a magazine due to lack of funding. And the poetry reading we had planned to hold for the other prisoners was canceled for reasons no one understood, least of all me.

"Mr. Cruz, when do you get out?" I asked. By this point, we all knew a lot about each other's personal lives, dire warnings notwithstanding. Only thing I didn't know was what they were in for, and how long they had left.

"Fourteen months," he said.

"And you'll have your bachelor's, right?"

"Yeah."

"You ever think about getting an MFA?"

He smiled. "You think so?"

"Yes, I do. You're a good writer, Mr. Cruz. And you'll only get better."

Mr. Cruz was light years ahead of any student I'd had in my classes I taught at the college. He was a voracious reader. Sensitive. And smart. When the class read the poem "Telemachus" by Ocean Voung, he said "Telemachus was Odysseus' son, right?" I said I had no idea. And he knew more about meter and rhyme than any teacher I had ever known, sometimes correcting me when I got things wrong.

When I had read a poem by former prisoner–poet Jimmy Santiago Baca, Mr. Cruz shook his head firmly and said "That's dope.

That poem right there. That's dope." He held the poem in his hands as they trembled, and I imagined he hoped his life going in the same direction: rebirth and reclamation.

"I'll write a letter of recommendation," I said. "Just ask me when you're ready."

I stood up and we shook hands. The intercom said it was time for a move up the hill.

"I would like that, Mr. Locke," he said.

"Chris," I said. "My name... is Chris."

Beacon

Lisa's surgery was awful; the doctor cut a small vein and the subsequent, unexpected repair was debilitating. Even now, a week out, she suffers trying to stand to go to the bathroom, cries out when rolling over in bed in hope some light from the window finds her face. It was enough to have six inches of her colon removed, but all this other subsequent bullshit has complicated everything for her. From waking and sitting, to merely breathing.

"Once you go through the procedure, you're going to notice a world of difference," her doctor said a while back. He's young. Cocky. And hasn't been right about a thing yet. Still, diverticulitis has wracked Lisa's insides, and she was desperate. Ever since she turned grey, started shaking, and collapsed onto the bed after wrapping the last present on Christmas Eve two years ago, her life has not been her own. I had to haul her out and into the car at 1:00 am, the girls too, and deliver her to the emergency room. I drove through a snowstorm, the flakes like dry sand flicking off my wipers, the girls confused and scared in their new Christmas Eve pajamas, both of them cold-chattering in the backseat.

That's when we first learned what had been making her feel so sick and weak for all those months, her stomach constantly stretched in fire and pain. She didn't come home that night, or even that week, and I drove the girls home through the same fucking snow to find our house cold and unlit. The girls climbed back up to bed even though it was after 6:00 am and they should have been well into their stockings by that point. The stockings remained hung on the mantel, bulging and indifferent.

I stood in front of the Christmas tree while drinking a pint glass of chardonnay and looked at all the ornaments, the handmade ones that were more beautiful for their sincerity and inexactitude: the corn husk angel bent and leaning high at the top; the picture of the girls smiling and framed in clumsy popsicle sticks. Presents flooded my ankles like an obscene joke.

But here we are now, side by side in the dark. And managing Lisa's pain has also been hard. Blue post-it notes run the length of a poetry journal like a crude message board detailing all the times she's due one med or another: is it Dilaudid now? No, no, wait, it's Ativan first. then Zofran. I check and recheck the times, afraid I'll overdose her.

It's also strange to have such a cache of opioids at my fingertips. So many ways to get high. I think about it when I'm rattling out her little white pills and they sound like delicious baton taps readying the music. Or when I hold the burnished prescription bottle in one hand and pop off the white cap with the other, so much treasure piled neat and clean at the bottom like tiny sacraments to God. It makes the whole mouth water.

But then I look at Lisa's face, her suffering, and realize I could never. What if I slipped a couple into my palm and washed them down in one glorious swallow? No harm, right? She has dozens. But what if it's those two she doesn't have access to when she runs out and she grimaces at me from the sheets wishing the pain would go away and all I can do is look down at her and repeat how sorry I am? No way. I could never do that to her.

I think.

Our house, which is over a hundred and forty years old, has become a beacon of suffering lately; a kind of lighthouse vibrating to anyone who might understand what it means to feel such hopelessness. Because not only has it been filled with Lisa's physical anguish, it has also been reverberating with our own personal misery; I'm moving out in a month, taking a job down in Virginia. The money was too good to refuse. Ostensibly, this move is about the job, but we have also been incapable of finding a bridge back to each other for some months now. The air of finality permeates everything.

Tonight, I woke up at 3:15. Lisa woke too. We both knew the other was up, but didn't say anything. I figured she was just ready for her next dose of Dilaudid, rising through the hard edges that narcotics otherwise soften.

I turned on the light and checked my meds list. I opened and shook bottles and handed her several different shaped pills. She took them while I held the glass of water. She said thank you. I turned off the light and lied back down next to her.

Everything was dark and quiet.

But something was off; I felt strangely scared, filled with a big scaredness I couldn't name or understand. I kept staring at the ceiling but had this awful sensation I was somewhere else, like waking between death and heaven. A place the lost inhabit when they don't know they're waiting to transition somewhere better. Or perhaps worse.

Come on, settle down, I thought. *You're tired and sleep has been spotty this week, Relax. Go back to sleep. Close your eyes.*

I closed my eyes.

"I'm scared," Lisa said.

"Why?"

"I don't know. Something is wrong and I can't stop dreaming. I keep dreaming but something is wrong."

She found my hand and held it.

"It's okay," I said.

Maybe it was the meds. With painkillers, I know how some people can't separate waking from sleeping, that everything coalesces into an indistinguishable otherness. God knows I've been there. But up to this point, Lisa hasn't shown any signs of this kind of disassociation or slippage. I wonder if it isn't the meds but it's us: our generalized fear has opened us up to receive a bad messenger, something evil taking advantage of our vulnerability. I think about my old church in New Hampshire and how some people became possessed by evil, that spirits would take advantage of helplessness and weakness and slide right in, a perfect fit.

I felt I was about to panic. True, authentic panic. That I had to suddenly get up and leave this house. Run down the road and not look back.

"Do you see those people?" Lisa whispered.

"What people?" My heart boomed like a canyon echo. I could feel my mouth run dry.

"There's a man and little boy standing in the doorway." Lisa's voice was like a child's.

I wanted to scream. Or cry. But I knew I had to look. In all that darkness, I simply had to look.

But then I thought, what if I see them too?

Voice

"All these words
for love... all these ways to say believe..."

—Reginald Dwayne Betts

For the last class I would ever teach in the prison, I took fourteen poems and laid them face down on a lacquered desk. Fourteen poems by fourteen poets. All pieces that matter to me, have helped shape my life in some way. I told my students to come up, one at a time, and grab the poem on the top, no peeking. I had no idea who would get which poem. I said read that poem in your hand to the class. Out loud. They did. Much starting and halting. Beginning again. Stopping again. *What does that word mean? Wait, this is about what?* After all of them completed their task, I said: Do not lose this poem. It is your poem. And by the end of the semester, you will recite this poem to me, and this class, by heart. It will have transformed into your own.

There's no way that's possible, said one. Others smiled while shaking their heads, glances catching other glances. Mr. Bellows, a former marine, stared at me as if trying to look right through me.

*   *   *

I had my students recite familiar songs and nursery rhymes in unsuspecting ways: "Mary Had A Little Lamb" in a whispering, evil voice; "Hickory Dickory Dock" as if terrified, looking back and forth over your shoulder; "Happy Birthday to You" sarcastically. Afterward, I asked what they remembered about the exercise.

"Yo, I seen Shorty bouncing around and shit like a creeper," said Mr. Hendricks, pointing at Mr. Macaya.

"Oh yeah," I said. "What else?"

"We were all acting like we were crazy," said Mr. Tuskey, a man from Chicago who was afraid parole would send him back to a community he no longer knew.

"You're right," I said. Then I turned and wrote "Attitude Over Aptitude" on the whiteboard. "Sometimes," I said, "It's not what you say, but how you say it."

*   *   *

The men were up practicing their descriptive speeches: describe someone, someplace, or something that impacted your life, good or bad.

Mr. Waters got up and spoke about his stepfather Red, a country western singer who played at Gilley's night club from *Urban Cowboy* fame. Mr. Waters remembers how he was allowed to sing with Red and put out a pickle jar for tips to a packed house. Mr. Waters was five and the audience ate it up. Later, as Red slipped deeper and deeper into alcoholism as his dreams of a gold record wouldn't materialize, he became increasingly abusive to Mr. Waters and his mother.

After years of torment, Mr. Waters, then twenty-one, went to visit Red for a promised night of drinking. He brought a case of beer and a fifth of Jack Daniels. At the end of the night, Mr. Waters went into the bathroom and took out a long hunting knife, ready to go back into the living room and kill Red. He looked in the mirror, breathed out once, and said "I'm ready." When he went back into the living room, Red was coughing hard and wet into a handkerchief. When he pulled it away, it was covered in blood.

"And that's when I knew God would do my work for me," Mr. Waters said to the class. So he sat down next to Red, patted his shoulder, and finished his beer instead.

Mr. Russell went next. He is a large man, shoulders like wide metal rollers in a factory. Wiry black beard, white kufi hat tight around his shaved head. He said on the night he was transferred to a new penitentiary fifteen years ago, his sat up listening to a man being raped in the darkness two cells down. His own cellmate just laid there, not saying a thing.

"He wouldn't talk to me. He wouldn't say a thing as this man cried for help. I kept thinking 'Why won't you say anything? What am I doing here?'"

Mr. Russell converted to Islam in the coming weeks and says it is the one thing that has saved him, even now. Afterward, I thanked the men. I told them they were growing more and more comfortable speaking in front of each other. That their stories were powerful, and they, courageous.

Packing up and getting ready for the move back up the hill, Mr. Kinney, who's a dazzling painter and has completed dozens of portraits of the men, utilizing different shades of violet to highlight their cheekbones, said "Mr. Locke, you're no CO. Because you know why? Because COs don't save lives." I didn't know how to respond, so I just said what you're supposed to say when given a gift: I thanked him.

*   *   *

Every class, between all the exercises, challenges and setbacks, small victories, the men practiced those poems I gave them. All fourteen. They studied. They spoke. They whispered their poems. They filled our small room with great sounds as they stretched those words into creation. Sometimes in groups. Sometimes to themselves. For Mr. Cortez, I rewrote many of the words to his poem "I Have Good News" by Tony Hoagland phonetically, as

English is his second language and he hadn't graduated high school in the Dominican Republic (a baseball career derailed at age sixteen).

There was much struggle for the men, there were many who quit, said they would try again, and then quit again. Only to again try.

But in our last class together, what power in their presentations. What ownership of language. These poems, all along, were more theirs than I even realized. Or planned.

Mr. Rialto, who previously had never read a poem in his life, joked before we started that Galway Kinnell's "Blackberry Eating" had become his poem of seduction. Of lust. "I recited it to my girl on the phone the other day, replaced blackberry with a very different word." He smiled. The men in class let out a satisfied howl.

And Mr. Waters, who bravely recited "To Myself" by Franz Wright. During the semester he informed me he was incarcerated for manufacturing and distributing meth, was an addict himself. He openly wept in class in front of the men during one of his speeches—the one about Red—as he thanked them all for being vulnerable, and for allowing him to be the same. When Mr. Waters said: "and the catastrophic dawn,/the nicotine crawling on your skin—/and when you begin/to cough I won't cover my face,/and if you vomit this time I will hold you:/everything's going to be fine" I believed him. The dignity in his face.

And Mr. Russell, who read Jim Daniels' "Wheels," about the speaker's brother always waving in photographs from behind the wheel of a car or truck or motorbike. We all learned in class just the other night that Mr. Russell's younger brother died at age thirteen because he snuck out in the family car and crashed at a hundred miles per hour. When Mr. Russell looked at us and said "my brother's feet/rarely touch the ground-/waving waving/face pressed to the wind/no camera to save him" we realized the poem was now a kaddish.

And Mr. Tuskey knew firsthand of the gangs in Chicago but vowed for something better for his two children when he gets out, read Kazim Ali's "Rain." And when he recited with such force "I am a dark bowl, waiting to be filled./If I open my mouth now, I could drown in the rain./I hurry home as though someone is there waiting for me./The night collapses into your skin. I am the rain." I was both thrilled and mesmerized because there could be no way he was lying.

And Mr. Cortez? He read every line of Hoagland's poem as a plea: "The dark ending does not cancel out/the brightness of the middle./Your day of greatest joy cannot be dimmed by any shame." And when he finished I put my hands together and filled the room with noise. As did the men. And we were happy then; bound together by something closer to love.

Christopher Locke was born in New Hampshire and received his MFA from Goddard College. His essays and short fiction have appeared in The *North American Review*, *The Sun*, *The Rumpus*, *Slice*, *JMWW*, *SmokeLong Quarterly*, *Barrelhouse*, and *Atticus Review*, among others. He won the Dorothy Sargent Rosenberg Poetry Award, as well as grants in poetry from the Massachusetts Cultural Council and the New Hampshire State Council on the Arts. *25 Trumbulls Road*, his first collection of fiction, won the Black River Chapbook Award. His latest collection of poetry *Music For Ghosts* (*NYQ Books*) was released in 2022. Chris lives in the Adirondacks and teaches English at SUNY Plattsburgh and North Country Community College.